MAKING CONTEMPORARY
WOODEN TABLES

MAKING CONTEMPORARY
WOODEN TABLES

18 ELEGANT PROJECTS FROM DESIGNER-CRAFTSMEN

THOMAS STENDER

LARK BOOKS

A Division of Sterling Publishing Co., Inc.
New York

Dedication

To my daughters, Elizabeth Jane and Abigail Rose, who will always have enough tables.

Art Direction and Production: **KATHLEEN HOLMES**
Senior Editor: **DEBORAH MORGENTHAL**
Production Assistance: **HANNES CHARIN**
Photography: **EVAN BRACKEN**
Additional Photography: **THOMAS STENDER, THOM ROUSE**
Illustrations: **THOMAS STENDER**

Library of Congress Cataloging-in-Publication Data
Stender, Thomas William, 1947-
    Making contemporary wooden tables : 18 elegant
projects from designer-craftsmen / Thomas Stender.—1st ed.
        p.   cm.
    Includes index.
    ISBN 1-57990-167-0 (paper)
    1. Tables. 2. Furniture making. 3. Woodwork.   I. Title.
TT197.5.T3 S72 2000
684.1'3—dc21   00-027457
                                CIP

10 9 8 7 6 5 4 3 2 1

First Edition

Published by Lark Books, a division of
Sterling Publishing Co., Inc.
387 Park Avenue South, New York, NY 10016

© 2000, Lark Books

Distributed in Canada by Sterling Publishing,
c/o Canadian Manda Group, One Atlantic Ave., Suite 105
Toronto, Ontario, Canada M6K 3E7

Distributed in Australia by Capricorn Link (Australia) Pty Ltd.,
P.O. Box 6651, Baulkham Hills Business Centre
NSW 2153, Australia

If you have any questions or comments about this book,
please contact:
Lark Books
50 College Street
Asheville, NC 28801
(828) 253-0467

Printed in Hong Kong.

ISBN 1-57990-167-0

Contents

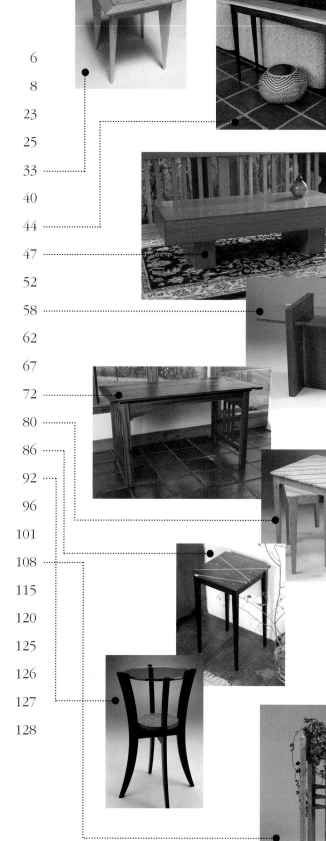

Introduction

Have you been looking for excellent table designs to build for your home? Have you wondered how professional woodworkers construct their furniture? Do you want to learn new skills by building challenging projects?

This book presents 18 wooden tables, designed by professional designer/craftsmen, with step-by-step instructions to help you build these pieces for your own home. If you have some experience with woodworking, you can find a suitable project here. Some may seem elementary to you, but others will challenge your skills and help you learn new ones. Some of the designs presented here are strikingly contemporary, while others draw upon familiar antecedents, from Shaker to Arts and Crafts to simply Modern. Most importantly, since the designs come from people who make furniture every day, these tables are designed to be built. And I will do my best to help you build them, too.

I have been designing and building furniture for 25 years. I guess you could say that I know my way around a shop. In talking with other experienced woodworkers, I have enjoyed the fact that all of them understand both the satisfaction and the frustration that working with wood delivers, often in equal measure. Our recognition that woodworking presents seemingly endless challenges tends to encourage generosity in sharing the knowledge we have won. That is certainly the case with those who have contributed their designs and their methods for this book.

I have also noticed that woodworkers tend to be amazingly inventive. They are mechanics, in the old, or rural, sense of the term: if the right part, tool, or material isn't available, they can probably find something that will do as well. If they need to make something, they will find a way to do it. Yet, while woodworkers tend to be independent thinkers, woodworking itself engenders a type of deep conservatism. We do not readily abandon methods that have worked well in the past, especially when so many previous failures led us to them. Every woodworker I know has tried at least three different ways of cutting dovetails to find the one which is incontrovertibly, absolutely, completely, the best way. For him or her.

There's another reason for this conservatism, as well. Almost all woodworking, and certainly furnituremaking, is additive: we carefully shape one piece of wood, to which we attach several more, in a way that makes it impossible to correct the first one, to arrive at a construction that readily reveals its flaws. So we try to work in ways that guarantee a good result.

Please forgive my philosophizing: my intention is to describe you, Gentle Reader, fine or aspiring craftsperson, seeker after truth, freedom, and the woodworking way.

YOU AND YOUR SHOP

I assume that you have some experience working with wood and with woodworking tools. I will guide you through the steps necessary to make each table, keeping parts and processes in order, helping you avoid pitfalls, and stopping occasionally to explain a difficult move. While the instructions are not written for beginners, I believe that anyone who has built some projects before, and who has a desire to learn more, can begin with some of the easier tables and progress to more difficult ones. Because this book is written for people with a wide range of skills and experience, some of the instructions may seem annoyingly elementary, or even condescending, to some readers. If, on occasion, you find that to be the case, I beg your forgiveness and urge you to read on. There's thrills aplenty in these pages.

As you read over the projects, you may think that I assume you have a fully-equipped shop. That is not necessarily the case. While I mention a number of power tools repeatedly, I assume that, if you lack that particular tool, you can find another way of doing its job. If you do not have a thickness planer, you might buy your lumber surfaced, or have it milled at an obliging shop. You might use a simple jig to help you bore an angled hole and stick some tape on the bit to tell you when to stop drilling. You might use a radial arm saw instead of a table saw (though the results may not be as accurate) and a saber saw instead of a band saw. Finally, you may

Thomas Stender, **Glowing Eye**, 1991; curly cherry, glass, gold leaf; 28" x 18" x 26"; photo by K. C. Kratt

be able to rent time in a fully-equipped shop or take a woodworking course that allows you access to machinery.

You won't find specific recommendations for tool brands here. Suffice it to say that more money buys better tools. Buy what you can afford and spend more on excellent edge tools, such as chisels and planes and a dozuki saw, even if that means putting off buying a better table saw. Remember that all tools need adjusting and sharpening from time to time. Better tools keep their edges and their accuracy longer. They increase the pleasure you get from woodworking by reducing the time you spend preparing to work wood.

While we're talking about pleasure, the more you learn about woodworking, the more fun it will be. So, even if you're sure you understand the topics covered in the next section, you might want to skim its contents to see if you can pick up something new. Please do read About the Projects. It contains important information about terminology and about the rights and responsibilities you've acquired with this book. Then, start building! I hope you do take pleasure in building these beautiful tables.

POWER TOOLS

Since you ask, here is a list of the power tools mentioned or assumed in the projects. I have arranged them in the order in which I would purchase them if I were starting from scratch. (Argue amongst yourselves—it's my list and I'm sticking to it.)

Circular saw

Biscuit jointer

Table saw

Jointer

Band saw

Thickness planer

Router

Drill press

Basic Knowledge for Table Builders

The following section contains a diverse group of tips, methods, and processes which are used in many of the projects. You may be familiar with some or all of these subjects, but I encourage you to at least scan the section to find out what's there. The discussion of these topics is intended to provide a common vocabulary, a basic set of special tools, for the instructions in the project section. The project instructions often refer to particular topics in this section, so you can also simply look up a topic when it's applicable.

However, please do read the short introduction to the project section. It contains important information about building the projects and understanding the instructions.

FLATTENING, THICKNESSING, AND JOINTING

This section explains how to prepare your stock before you begin using it in any project. Even if you think you know everything I can possibly say here, please read it anyway. It's only a few paragraphs. Then we'll both know that we have good material to work with. If you don't read this section, believe me, I'll insert it at the beginning of every project in the book.

Many of the projects in this book call for stock planed to thicknesses other than the ¾" and 1½" common in softwood lumber. The designers have tried to be sensitive to the visual weight of the various elements of their tables, using thicknesses that specifically complement their intentions in the design. Before you surface your material or have it done for you,

YOU MUST FLATTEN IT FIRST!

I'm sorry to shout, but this is important. If you simply surface a bowed or twisted plank, you will end up with a bowed or twisted plank that is all the same thickness. These conditions do not lead naturally to good work.

Hardwoods are generally sold as rough (unplaned) planks of variable widths in thicknesses called ¼, ⅝, ¾, ⅞, etc., and pronounced "four-quarter,

five-quarter," etc. Your supplier may be willing to surface your material for you or may sell it already surfaced. In the latter case, you must choose your planks very carefully for flatness. That bow or cup will not magically disappear on the way home. If the supplier discourages picking, you should leave and tell him why: you are not being well served. If you do pick through a stack of lumber, however, make very sure that you leave the stack looking at least as good as it did when you started.

You may not own a thickness planer, but you should own, or have access to, a jointer. Begin the process of preparing your stock by cutting it into convenient lengths, somewhat longer than the finished sizes. Do not cut lengths shorter than 24" or so. Instead, group small pieces in longer lengths that are easier and safer to handle. You will begin planing by flattening one surface of each piece. Inspect each board to see how it curves and to determine the direction of the grain. Generally, it is best to begin by flattening the concave surface. If you think that there is no concave surface, look harder. You will need to run this face over the jointer several times until its entire surface is clean. This gives you an accurate reference plane for all subsequent operations. If the board chatters and you see excessive tear-out, reverse the direction of the board. If that doesn't work, sharpen the jointer knives. Set the depth of cut fairly shallow so that you do not remove any more wood than is necessary. Before going on to the next board, joint one edge straight and square to the flattened surface. Sight along the sharp edge to make sure that it's straight. A slightly concave line is acceptable.

Now your material is ready for thicknessing. If you own a thickness planer, proceed. If you do not, you will have to find someone to thickness your stock. In either case, make sure that you plane with the grain (see Some Relevant Terminology on page 23.) and that you begin flipping the board lengthwise as soon as the second face is clean. Flipping the board with each pass through the planer ensures that an equal amount of wood is removed from each side

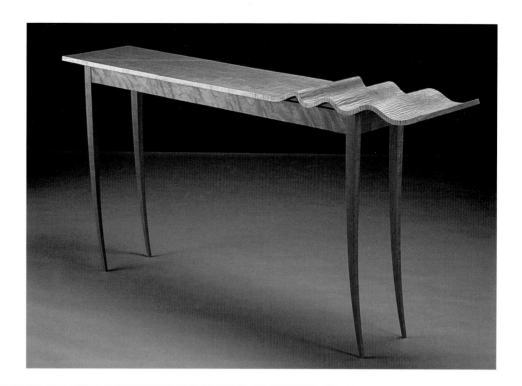

Thomas Stender,
Wave Goodbye, 1987;
curly maple, curly cherry;
61" x 12" x 31";
photo by K. C. Kratt

of the plank, lessening the chance that the board will cup due to stresses within the plank.

Once it has been reduced to the proper thickness, the material is ready to be ripped to its finished width. Boards to be glued together for a table top should be ripped to the greatest width that produces a straight edge. Then arrange the planks as they will be glued together. Tops tend to look more attractive and are easier to sand if the grain goes the same direction on all planks, but your first priority should be a pleasing overall grain pattern. Draw a diagonal pencil line across all the boards to show their positions.

Now pick up each board in turn and joint its right edge and then its left edge, leading with the same end every time. This procedure ensures that you will end up with a flat table top even if your jointer fence is not set at exactly 90° to the infeed table. At any fence angle, you will cut complementary angles, which, for this particular job, are necessary for a flat top. You will probably see a small opening in the middle of each edge joint when you push the jointed boards together. If the boards are slightly and evenly concave along their edges, the joint will close easily with fewer clamps. However, if you need too much clamp pressure to pull the boards together, you can introduce so much stress in the top that cured glue will be pushed out of the joints months later, resulting in barely visible, but annoying, ridges at the joints.

KEEPING TABLE TOPS FLAT

Should you alternate the direction of annular rings when gluing up a table top or other wide panel from solid wood? Unaccountably left unanswered by philosophers, this question has bedeviled woodworkers for ages. But here, at last, is the answer: No. Usually.

We all know that wood expands at right angles to the grain as it takes on moisture and shrinks as it dries. Because of this, we have learned to allow for this inevitable movement by using frame-and-panel construction, for instance, or by using oversized screw holes to hold table tops. Unfortunately, expansion and shrinkage do not happen evenly throughout a plank unless it's truly quarter-sawn. The side of any plain-sawn plank that was farther from the center of the tree expands and contracts more than the side that was closer to the center.

Look at the end-grain of any plain-sawn plank. It's easy to see where the center of its tree-of-origin must have been. While you're looking, imagine the annular rings as concentric rows of equal-sized cells, which, in fact, they are. The cells of each ring, having been born at about the same time, like to stick together and move as one. And each year more cells were added than were born the year before, because they had to surround the previous bunch. When the cells in the board take a drink, each one swells and elbows its brothers. Because there are more cells in

Gary Peterson,
Koa Coffee Table,
1978; koa, ebony;
42" x 22" x 18";
photo by Gary Peterson

the rings toward the outside of the tree, those rings expand more than the adjacent inside rings. Therefore, the board becomes convex on the face toward the outside of the tree. If the board gets drier than it was when it was flat, the outside face becomes concave. These expanding and contracting forces are quite strong.

When we glue two or more planks edgewise, they tend to act as one plank. When all of the planks in a table top have all their annular rings going the same way, they act as if they were one, very wide plain-sawn board. If they get wetter, they will form one arched surface. This would seem to be an inappropriate condition for a table top, but it isn't because we can apply enough leverage, with screws through rails, to keep that gently curved surface flat. Think of it this way: a cupped board, 5" wide, is lying on a table concave side down. Can you exert enough downward force to flatten that board? Probably not. But if you pushed down on a 30"-wide board, cupped to the same arc, you could produce a pretty flat surface.

When planks are glued together with alternating annular rings, and they get wetter or drier, they form a wavy surface which is harder for screw pressure to control. You would need to drive many more screws to keep that table flat.

So the general rule is this: Under usual circumstances, with a well-supported table top, align the annular rings of all the planks in the same way. When a top will be difficult to control because of its thickness or inadequate support, alternate the rings and use relatively narrow boards.

GLUING TABLE TOPS

There are only three things that can go wrong when you're gluing up boards to make a table top. The boards can stick together at different levels, requiring a lot of belt-sanding to make a flat (and thinner) top. The top can come out bowed so much that sanding to flatten it would reduce the edges to slivers. And the joints may not glue together, leaving cracks in the joints or openings at the ends of the table. This last problem results from poor jointing: either the edges of the boards were bumpy or convex, or they were so concave that the glue couldn't hold them together. The other two faults can be avoided in the gluing process.

Bowed tops come from bad clamping, assuming that you follow good jointing practice as outlined above, producing complementary angles on your edges. Pipe

Photo 1

John Bickel,
***Glengary Game
Table and Chairs***,
1995; mahogany;
32" x 32" x 29";
photo by John Bickel

clamps pull boards together wonderfully, but they bend fairly easily. You can get the pressure points of a pipe clamp lined up perfectly inside the thickness of the clamped top, but the pipe will bend as you apply pressure, changing the angles of the clamp heads or simply pushing the middle of the pipe into the middle of the table top. This happens to a lesser extent with long bar clamps and beam clamps, too.

Applying pipe clamps in alternating order presents a partial solution, but you still must make sure to balance the pressure between the clamps on the top and the clamps on the bottom. That's why double pipe clamp fixtures (photo 1 on page 26) are invaluable for gluing wide panels. When you flop them so that both pipes lie against the wood, they apply consistent pressure through the center of the panel.

The problem of alignment in edge gluing can be solved mechanically by using biscuits in problem areas (see Biscuit Joinery on page 16). Use biscuits only when and where necessary and do not glue them; they can produce local areas of the "glue creep" described above. The glue on the edges of the planks will hold the top together. Most of the time, however, you can align the boards very well during the clamping process by applying pressure gradually. Here's where the slightly concave edges that are a natural result of jointing come in very handy. After applying

glue to the edges and pushing the boards together, clamp them lightly (and only near the ends if this is a long top). Make sure that the ends of the boards align first, gradually tightening the clamps and moving your attention toward the center of the panel. In this way you can adjust the alignment in smaller areas of the panel, essentially clamping each section as you go.

FASTENING TABLE TOPS

Having experience with wood, you know that it expands and contracts across the grain with changes in humidity. The movement can be quite dramatic: a 10"-wide piece of flat-sawn cherry will commonly lose ⅛" or more of width wintering in a northern house and gain it back the next summer. (This does not mean, romantics, that the wood is "alive.") Additionally, the force of the wood's movement can push joints apart and pull screws out. You must accommodate this movement or risk damage to your project. Fastening table tops presents particular challenges because they can be quite wide.

Most of the common means for letting the top slide on its base are used in one or more of the projects in this book. There is no best method, only what may work best in a particular situation. Read through the projects to discover ways of fastening that may not have occurred to you.

DROP STOPS, JIGS, AND FIXTURES

I've grouped these three items together because they all help us work more accurately, more efficiently, and more safely. Most of us, when we began working with wood and buying tools, assumed that each tool we bought would solve our problems, both physical and emotional. Gradually, we realized that every new chisel needs sharpening and every new machine needs adjusting. That led many of us to invent attachments that expand the capabilities of the machines. And a few people continued on this dark road until they did no woodworking except for making gadgets to facilitate (eventual) woodworking. Avoid that path if you can, Gentle Reader, as there looms madness. We must all determine for ourselves whether making a jig to make the work go faster will take longer than simply making the work.

One such gizmo is a no-brainer: the *drop stop*. Commonly used on table saws and radial arm saws, the drop stop allows us to cut the same length repeatedly, and flips out of the way when we need to cut something else. If a drop stop came with your miter gauge, you're all set. If one is available for your miter gauge, go buy it now. If not, you can achieve the same results by clamping a scrap to your miter gauge fence. Cut an end off every board from which you intend to cut pieces of the same length (photo 2), drop or clamp the stop in place, and start sawing, placing each squared end against the stop (photo 3).

I often use the drop stop even when I have only one cut to make because I can measure directly from the stop to the blade, eliminating the step of marking the edge of the board. In addition, by setting the drop stop first and flipping it out of the

way for the first cut, I can turn on the table saw once to make both cuts.

You can extend the usefulness of the drop stop for making incremental cuts, such as a series of equally spaced dados, by making a set of identical blocks, each the length of the interval between the cuts. Put one block against the stop to make a second cut, say 1" away from the first. Add another block to cut 2" away. You get the idea.

A *jig* is mechanism that allows us to do a particular job more easily. The taper jig shown in photos 4 and 5 offers a good example of an efficient jig. It can be made in less time than it would take to mark out the eight cuts we need to make for the project. Furthermore, cutting with the jig on the table saw yields faster and more accurate results than cutting freehand on the band saw.

A *fixture* allows us to hold a workpiece while we machine it. The fixture illustrated in figure 1 on page 117 consists of a stack of plywood shaped to hold a curved apron for the Bent Apron Table so that we can cut the workpiece to length and cut mortises in its ends. The question of efficiency rarely arises with fixtures—they simply must be made for particular, usually curved, pieces.

FAIR CURVES AND PATTERNS

A *fair curve* is one without humps and hollows. An *arc of a circle* and a *french curve* are fair curves. Boatbuilders take fair curves very seriously and spend many hours fairing (smoothing) a hull so that it doesn't disturb the water flowing past it any more than necessary. If you've seen a curved table leg that

Photo 2

Photo 3

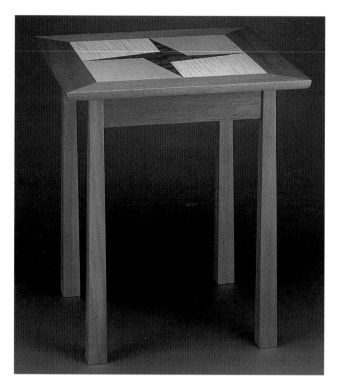

Ron Trumble, **End Table—Mosaic,** 1999; maple, birdseye maple, English sycamore; 20" x 20" x 22"; photo by George Post

Ron Trumble, **Quilted Series—Star**, 1999; mahogany, quilted maple, makore, black-dyed veneer, ebony; 20" x 20" x 24"; photo by George Post

looked ugly to you, it may have had a curve which changed too abruptly or had an unwanted recurve. These are examples of unfair curves. I like to sketch a new, curved leg or apron first, often right on the pattern stock; but neither you nor I can draw a fair curve freehand. No collection of french curves and ship's curves will always provide something suitable to trace. We need to use a batten.

A *batten* is the most useful tool for describing a fair curve. Battens occur in many sizes and materials, and you can't buy one—you must find it or make it. A batten must bend smoothly, so it can be made of any homogenous material which returns to its previous shape after bending. I have a three-foot aluminum ruler which makes a great batten for shallow curves, both because it bends nicely and because I have somehow kept it from getting kinked. Boatbuilders

Photo 4

Photo 5

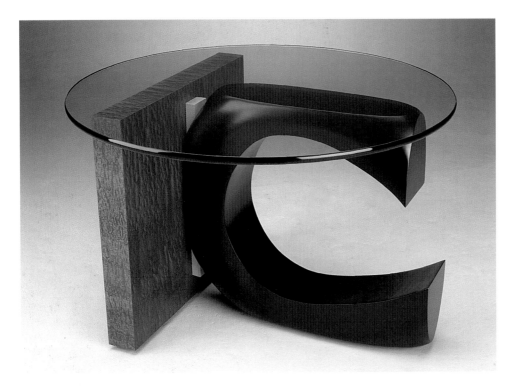

Richard Judd, *Omega Table,* 1998; poplar with black lacquer, pomele sapele veneer, MDF, glass; 28" x 28" x 22"; photo by Bill Lemke

typically make battens from very straight-grained soft-woods so that they can change the shape and thickness for a particular curve. You can easily tell if a batten is too stiff for the job at hand, but beware of a batten which is too flexible. A too-weak batten won't bridge "hard spots," leaving bumps in the curve. Try drawing a shallow, fair curve with a strip of paper.

All of which is a long way of saying that you will have to find or make a suitable batten for any fair curve you wish to draw. Remember: it must have no curvy tendencies of its own and it must want to return to its straight condition.

Photo 6 shows a batten being used to draw the leg pattern for Move Over on page 25. I have clamped my aluminum ruler to a block of wood representing the joint area, which must remain straight. That block in turn is clamped securely to the pattern stock and to the table, holding everything in place. I have marked some guide points along the curve, based on the grid illustration on page 26, and I have sketched the curve. My left hand bends the ruler to a fair curve. Notice that I have bent the ruler past the bottom end of the leg. If I simply push the ruler over to the bottom point of the leg, as in photo 7, the curve will flatten toward that end instead of becoming more

Photo 6

Photo 7

Thomas Stender,
Sweet Dislocation,
1988; curly cherry;
30" x 19" x 24";
photo by K. C. Kratt

rounded, as it should. When I am pleased with the curve, I trace the line with a sharp pencil with light sideways pressure to avoid moving the batten with the pencil.

Notice that I trace the line on the inside of the ruler, the side that will be the leg. Then I saw to the outside of that line and use a low-angle block plane or a spokeshave to smooth the sawn edge while leaving the pencil line on the pattern stock. Making the pattern the exact size of the leg allows me to saw the leg one pencil-width outside of the pattern, leaving just enough extra wood to be able to smooth the leg down to the pattern size. Isn't that convenient?

You can make patterns from many materials, but I find matte board, good-quality thin plywood, and thicker plywood most useful, each in its own way. Since you cut matte board with a knife, you can use a ruler to get perfectly straight lines, but mistakes on curved lines are hard to correct. Matte board bends easily, so you can trace a pattern onto a curved surface, but it's too flexible for narrow shapes. When following a line with the knife, draw the knife along

at a low angle without much pressure. Cut through with successive passes once you've made a good path for the knife to follow.

Thin plywood makes good patterns for flat or slightly curved workpieces and for skinny shapes. Cut to the pencil line with a band saw, then smooth the edges with a low-angle block plane and/or a spokeshave. This step allows you to correct any mistakes made with the band saw, and it gives you another chance to make sure that you've drawn fair curves. Run the length of your finger and hand along the edge, trying to detect any hills and valleys.

You'll need thicker plywood if you intend to use the pattern with a ball-bearing guided flush cutter on a router or shaper. You make it in the same way as you would with thinner material, but saw outside the line traced on the workpiece instead of to the line. Affix the pattern to the workpiece with double-sided tape (carpet tape works well), and use the flush cutter to trim the workpiece to the precise shape of the pattern. Clearly, any mistakes on the pattern will show up on every piece made with it.

Thomas Stender,
Just Weave,
1989; satinwood,
wenge, ebonized
walnut; 64" x 12"
x 30"; photo by K.
C. Kratt

BISCUIT JOINERY

All of the professional woodworkers I know use biscuit joinery. Many amateur woodworkers remain resistant to using biscuits, and that is a shame. In my opinion, biscuit joinery, which became widely accepted in the 1980's, is simply the most important small-shop woodworking invention of the century and the first real advancement in mortise-and-tenon joinery in many centuries. This system allows all of

us to make strong, all-wood, invisible joints, even in situations where traditional joints are nearly impossible. Still, many workers believe that a mortise-and-tenon joint must be stronger than a joint made with a small scrap of wood. Admittedly, there are situations (post-and-beam barns, for instance) where biscuits won't work, but for normal woodworking they have plenty of strength.

The *biscuit joint* consists of matching slots filled with a manufactured spline. The grain in the spline, or biscuit, runs diagonally to the joint, so it resists splitting. It consists of hardwood (usually beech) which has been compressed to a sliding fit in the slots. When water-based glue, such as yellow woodworking glue, contacts the biscuit, it swells to fill the width of the slot completely. This produces a very strong joint because it maximizes friction within the wood and leaves a large shoulder area to resist racking.

The tool which cuts the slots consists of a motor driving a 4"-diameter cutter which looks and acts just like a small circular saw blade (see photo 8). A spring-loaded base encloses the cutter so that pushing the motor forward while the front of the base is against a piece of wood pushes the cutter into the wood. The blade cuts a slot shaped like the profile

Photo 8

Ron Trumble,
Coffee Table,
1995; cherry, bird-
seye maple, ebony,
black-dyed veneer;
18" x 46" x 16";
photo by George Post

of half a football. Three depth settings are provided for the three sizes of biscuits available. An adjustable and tiltable fence allows cutting at varying distances from the surface of the workpiece and cutting slots at angles or into angled surfaces.

Making a typical biscuit joint goes like this: Place the two pieces of wood together as you wish to join them. With a pencil, mark the center of the joint area across the joint onto both pieces. Adjust the depth fence on the tool so that the slot will be approximately centered in the wood. Align the center mark on the tool with the pencil line on one piece, turn on the tool, and push the cutter smoothly into the wood. Repeat this process on the other workpiece. Put yellow glue in both slots. Push a biscuit into one slot and push the two workpieces together, aligning the pencil lines. Apply a clamp for a few minutes. You've just made an extremely strong mortise and tenon joint. Ain't technology swell?

Here's a table showing the dimensions of the three sizes of slots and biscuits:

Biscuit #	Biscuit length	Biscuit width	Slot length	Slot depth
0	$1\frac{7}{8}$"	$\frac{5}{8}$"	$2\frac{1}{8}$"	$\frac{3}{8}$"
10	$2\frac{1}{16}$"	$\frac{3}{4}$"	$2\frac{3}{8}$"	$\frac{7}{16}$"
20	$2\frac{1}{4}$"	$\frac{7}{8}$"	$2\frac{5}{8}$"	$\frac{1}{2}$"

As you can see, the two slots in a joint have $\frac{1}{8}$" extra depth allowance for glue. If both edges of what would be the tenoned piece are going to be visible, then that piece must be wider than the slot length. It must be, say, $2\frac{1}{2}$" wide, if you're using #10 biscuits. However, where you can hide one edge of the joint, as under a table top, you can let the slots and biscuit run past that edge and trim the biscuit flush. See the Outdoor Stacking Tables on p. 80 for an example of this method.

Biscuit joints will work anywhere you might use a mortise-and-tenon joint, but they have many other uses as well. All the joints in a bookcase, for instance, may be replaced with biscuits, even dovetailed corners. When you need help aligning edge joints in large table tops, use a biscuit where necessary. In this case, there's no real need to glue the biscuits, since the glued edge joint should be strong enough by itself. In other words, don't expect biscuits to hold an otherwise suspect joint together.

The projects in this book contain examples of several ways of indexing, or properly aligning, biscuit slots. When joining small workpieces, it's common to put the biscuit jointer upside down in a bench vice. This way, you can hold the work to the fence and push it into the cutter. Your biscuit jointer will have marks on its base to aid positioning the work, and you can add your own for particular applications, as in the Outdoor Stacking Tables project.

Left: Ron Trumble, ***Breakfast Table***, 1992; makore, birdseye maple, holly, ebony; 40" x 40" x 30"; photo by George Post

Right: Richard Judd, ***Table with Edge Inlay***, 1989; curly maple, wenge; 19" x 19" x 26"; photo by Bill Lemke

Far right: Richard Judd, ***Carved Leg Table***, 1996; carved poplar, black lacquer, lacewood, glass; 24" x 24" x 21"; photo by Bill Lemke

For work between ⅜" and ⅞" thick, you may omit the fence, simply using the surface of your bench instead. Hold the work piece with one hand or a clamp and push the cutter in with the other hand. For thicker pieces, or to move the slot to produce an offset between the two sides of the joint, use spacers between the bench and the biscuit jointer. Both of these methods are employed in the Centered Square Table project (page 33).

SIMPLE VENEERING

Several of the projects incorporate a small, veneered panel. Many lumber outlets offer at least some plywood with nice, hardwood face veneers, but you may want to use a more interesting wood. While a full discussion of veneering is well beyond the scope of this book, I will describe a relatively uncomplicated method for applying veneer in small doses. With a little preparation, you can lay up the panels required for these projects, even if you have never worked with veneer before.

You can eliminate a number of potential problems by choosing suitable material. First, make sure that the veneer is fairly flat. Pronounced bubbles and wrinkles don't press out readily and can lead to splits when you try to flatten them. Second, try to buy a piece of veneer large enough to cover your panel. That saves splicing and taping. Still, you can joint the edges of pieces

under 24" long rather easily. When the edges fit together well, tape across the joint on the good side with paper veneer tape, regular masking tape, or, better, plastic masking tape that stretches a bit. After gluing, peel off the masking tape or sand off the paper tape.

Many glues work for small panels. I often use yellow woodworking glue on pieces under 24" square, but I make sure to press the sandwich quickly so that the expanding veneer doesn't overlap at a joint. Epoxy works very well except that it often penetrates the veneer and spreads out over the surface. Sanding won't eliminate the resultant blotchiness, so I generally coat the good side with epoxy as well, and sand it smooth. This produces a very hard surface that shows sanding scratches, so sand carefully and well. Whatever you do, don't use contact adhesive with veneer. Contact cement remains flexible, allowing veneer to expand and contract until it comes loose. Contact cement is fine for plastic laminates, but not for fine furniture.

Finally, you can use substantial clamping pads instead of a "real" veneer press. Clamping pads, in this case, means pieces of plywood or MDF thick enough to distribute the pressure of your clamps over the whole panel. Determine the thickness of the pads you'll need by considering the size of the panel to be veneered and the size of your clamps. Figure that a clamp's pressure radiates in a 90° cone—pressure applied to a pad of ¾" plywood pushes effectively on

a 1½"-diameter circle on the other side of the plywood. If you own only narrow clamps, it may be time to buy some larger ones, because a small clamp depth limits you to pressing only the edges of the panel. On the other hand, a 5"-deep bar clamp, working with 5"-thick pads, can press half of a 20"-wide panel. So much for theory. Use the deepest clamps you can, use as many as you have, with 3"-thick pads top and bottom, and you'll produce a fine panel for any of the projects here. Except one: you would need a store-full of large clamps to veneer the panels for the Low Fat Table (page 47) using this method.

STRUCTURAL EPOXY

If you haven't used structural epoxy, you ought to try it. Not the glue you buy in small tubes at the drug store, structural epoxy is made for large jobs and has many uses in a furniture shop. Epoxy is an extremely strong adhesive made effectively stronger by its ability to fill gaps. If you have made a joint of questionable integrity, you can use epoxy instead of yellow glue and sleep soundly tonight.

Structural epoxy is widely used in boatbuilding because it forms a waterproof bond. The various demands for adhesives, fillers, and finishes in boat construction have spurred the development of complete systems of resins, hardeners, additives, and application products by several manufacturers. In return, boatbuilders have expanded the ways in which they use epoxy to the extent that some boats have almost no metal-to-wood fastenings in their hulls.

You buy epoxy in one-gallon, five-gallon, or 50-gallon kits, consisting of resin and hardener, although a trial-size kit may be available. Most manufacturers sell pumps that deliver the correct ratio of resin and hardener, making mixing the two much easier. You mix the epoxy by putting an equal number of pumps in a plastic pot and stirring well. Since the glue cures by an exothermic reaction, both the temperature of your shop and the size of your mixing tub affect its working time. If you pour the mixed epoxy into a roller pan (effectively spreading it so it can stay cooler) on a cool day, you will be able to work with the mixture for a longer period of time, maybe 30 minutes. Fast and slow hardeners extend your control over its working time.

When you mix it, epoxy is a thin liquid, suited to penetrating wood. In fact, so much of the glue can soak into porous woods that it leaves the joint "starved." Except for clear-coating, most applications require some additive to help the epoxy stay in a glue joint, to change its working properties, or to give it varying properties when it cures. You can easily change its uncured viscosity and its cured density, for instance. For general laminating, I use a small amount of microfibers in the epoxy mixture.

Left: Thomas Stender, **Rift**, 1993; cherry, glass, gold leaf; 60" x 14" x 30"; photo by K. C. Kratt

Right: John Bickel, **Console Table**, 1988; walnut, rosewood; 60" x 15" x 36"; photo by John Bickel

Microfibers are cotton fibers chopped to the consistency of fluffy powder. Spread the epoxy onto both surfaces to be joined using a short foam roller. You need to wet out the whole surface with a thin layer of glue, going back to those areas that begin to look dry. (See photo 9, where I am spreading glue on plywood and foam for the Low Fat Table.)

Clamp with enough pressure to close the joint. Epoxy requires only moderate clamping pressure because of its gap-filling abilities. You need not attain an especially thin glue line. This makes epoxy a very good

adhesive for veneer, its disadvantage being its thin viscosity, which allows it to soak through many veneers and puddle on the surface. You can minimize unwanted migration by pre-coating the glue surface of the veneer with epoxy and letting it cure. For best results, glue the veneer to its substrate within 24 hours, before the cured epoxy forms a film (referred to as "bloom") which can reduce the quality of subsequent glue bonds.

Here's a good example of epoxy's strength. I use biscuits glued with epoxy to join my chairs, with two spaced biscuits in each joint. Even though the chairs I design are joined only at the seat, I have not seen a failure in 12 years. To learn more about the possibilities epoxy offers for your furnituremaking, obtain the technical manuals from manufacturers. One of them publishes a book about boat construction which contains a wealth of information about gluing and coating wood.

BURNISHED OIL FINISH

You're probably wondering already what kind of finish to use on your table. For maximum protection, you might brush on several coats of polyurethane, carefully sanded between coats. With that kind of hard, surface finish, it's difficult to achieve a smooth last coat, free of dust, hair, brush strokes, sags, drips, gnats.... You get the point. You might spray lacquer if

Photo 9

you have the equipment, ventilation, and expertise. You may be able to pay a professional finisher to do the job for you.

If you want to do it yourself, as simply as possible, and still get a good shine, I recommend a burnished oil finish. This method uses polymerizing oil and paste wax and minimal elbow grease to produce a reasonable moisture barrier and a sheen which can be adjusted to suit your preference. It repairs easily and, best of all, dust and cat hairs can't ruin the last coat.

The secret to success with all finishes is sanding. Finishes tend to accentuate imperfections instead of covering them. In addition, the frayed fiber-ends left from rough sanding obscure the definition and color of the wood grain you're trying to display. So sand, sand, sand, remembering to remove all the scratches made by the previous grit with the very next finer grit you use.

Several oil finish products are available called antique oil finish or Danish oil finish or something similar.

Look for one with a high non-volatile materials content (over 30 percent) and which recommends wiping within 30 minutes. You will, of course, disregard the instructions on the can and follow mine to the letter.

Remove any dust from all the surfaces and from your work table. Wearing disposable latex gloves will keep the oil off your hands, a very good thing. Using a 1½" or 2" foam brush, coat the surface liberally, going back over any "dry" areas where the oil has soaked in. Don't apply more finish than you will be able to wipe off in about five minutes. Now wait for the oil to thicken. That may take five minutes or 30 minutes, depending on the oil, the wood, heat, and humidity. You want to wipe it off while you can do so easily, before it gets sticky, but if you wipe too soon you'll wipe off too much potential finish. If the oil gets too sticky to wipe, apply a thin coat of fresh oil and wipe immediately. Use a brand of paper towels that holds together and doesn't leave lint. Keep replacing the towels with fresh ones, and keep wiping until the surface is dry. I mean dry. Completely. Even in the corners.

Thomas Stender,
A Broken Ground, 1992;
cherry, gold leaf;
42" x 22" x 18";
photo by K. C. Kratt

Those oil-laden towels and your brush will self-ignite if they are allowed to build up enough heat. One brand tells you to dispose of them in a closed metal container filled with water, presenting some physical and logistical problems. If you throw them in a large metal waste basket placed away from other flammables, at least until the oil cures, you should be okay. When the towels are completely dry, they are nearly as safe as other paper. Please take these warnings seriously.

Woods with open pores, such as oak and wenge and sometimes mahogany, let oil droplets seep back onto the surface as the oil oxidizes and warms. Try to wipe off those droplets as they appear. If you miss some, remove them with 0000 steel wool (that's "four aught") before you apply another coat. While you're at it, look for any areas you might have skipped while wiping. Rub those smooth as well. Did I forget to tell you to wipe everything dry? No.

Apply a second coat the next day. Use less oil, but make sure you wet the surfaces completely. This coat and subsequent ones will thicken more quickly than the first, so test it often with a fingertip. Again, wipe everything completely dry. On the third day, do all that again. If your shop is warm and dry, you can apply the third coat after 12 hours, but only if the second coat is thoroughly dry.

Allow a day of drying time, then burnish the surfaces with 0000 steel wool. Rub hard with the grain of the wood until the surface feels very smooth and you can see an even, soft shine. Rub every bit of the finish, even if you have to rub cross-grain in the corners. You will end up with a very soft luster that looks a little dry.

To make the finish warmer, shinier, and more protective against spills, use a good-quality paste wax. I use a commercially available wax that is specially formulated for dark woods. You can use this on light woods, too, unless you want to retain the lightest possible color. Look for a paste wax that is fairly hard in the can. Use a pad of cheesecloth to rub it on across the grain first, finishing with light, even strokes with the grain. In only a few minutes the wax will be ready for buffing. Find an old t-shirt—or something similarly soft and porous—and rub vigorously until you get an even shine. Again, finish rubbing along the grain. If the wax gloss appears too shiny for you, dull it with light steel wool strokes carefully aligned along the grain.

This finish will withstand occasional washing with soap and water. When it begins to look dull, paste wax again. If water sits on a table top too long, it will leave a ring of lighter, raised grain. Rub this area hard with steel wool, reapply as many coats of oil as seem necessary, burnish, and rewax.

TABLE PROJECTS

About the Projects

The designs for the projects in this book were contributed by professional designer-craftsmen, a significant portion of whose income derives from producing and selling the furniture they design. Each of them has granted you, as purchaser of this book, the right to make *one* table of each design *for your own use only*. If you were to sell even that one table, you would be stealing from them just as surely as they would be if they came to your house and took a chair from your dining room. Don't do it.

Each project lists the materials used in the table pictured. In some cases, I have indicated alternative materials. You should feel free to substitute materials, with careful consideration of how they will affect the appearance of the table. Next comes a short list of supplies. These are generally items you may have already, but some may need to be ordered, such as the glass for the Glass-Top T Table.

The cutting list shows all the parts in each project. Its title does not mean that you should start cutting. Successful woodworking involves careful strategy, and sometimes cutting to length is the last, not the first, operation performed on a particular piece. You should always read all of the instructions for a project before you even start assembling your materials. Then follow them in order. I have carefully sequenced the steps to help you achieve a good result. Not every step depends on the previous one, it's true, but deviate from their order at your own risk.

The occasional table called Move Over comes first in this section because it includes many of the operations used in the other projects. I encourage you to read this project, including the sections in Basic Knowledge for Table Builders to which it refers, even if you do not intend to make Move Over. It will provide a functional introduction to the rest of the tables in the book.

SOME RELEVANT TERMINOLOGY

The dimensions listed in the cutting lists and throughout the book show the thickness first, the width second, and the length third. *Width* always means across the grain, while *length* always indicates the long-grain dimension. If you cut 1" off the end of a 2 x 4, that chunk would measure 1½" x 3½" x 1".

This book uses names for the parts of boards in particular and consistent ways, too. *Face* refers to a wide, long-grain side: width is measured across the face. *Edge* refers to a narrow long-grain side, where thickness is measured. *End* is the end-grain side, of course. *Corners* are where any two or three sides intersect, so *end corners* are the sharp places where faces and edges meet an end. And *ease the corners* means sand the corners slightly round so they're more friendly to your hand.

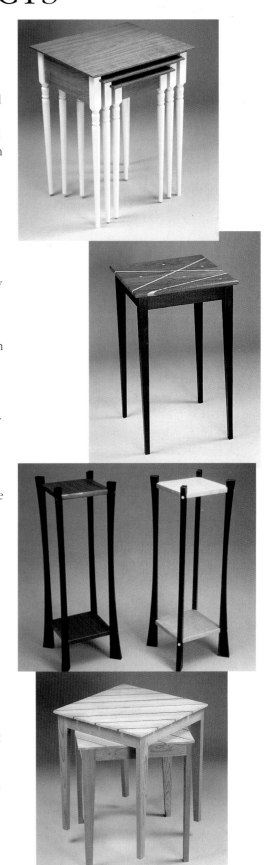

Finally, *with the grain* doesn't mean simply along the length of the board. In woodworking parlance there are two dichotomies: with/across and with/against. To avoid this confusion, I generally say *along the grain* as the opposite of *across the grain*. That leaves *with the grain* to mean, approximately, *in the easier direction*, akin to *with the flow*.

There are several ways to tell grain direction. You can look at the edge of the board; you can run your fingers over the surface; or, as happens all too often, you can find out the hard way.

Looking: If you look at the edge of a plank, you see a cross-section of the grain. Usually, the grain lines will not run straight along the plank but will tend to move upward or downward as they go from left to right. Here is a drawing of the grain lines on the edge of a board, with the grain direction indicated:

Feeling: If you run your fingers lightly along the surface of the wood, usually you can feel a smooth direction and a rougher direction in which the fibers seem to catch on your skin. The smooth direction is with the grain.

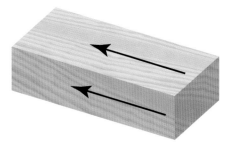

Hard Way: Often the grain lines don't read easily: they are curved, or wavy, or they simply lie. If your plane (or planer) breaks off chunks of wood, leaving the surface choppy instead of smooth, you are going against the grain in that area. You should first make sure that the plane iron is sharp and set properly. Then try planing in the opposite direction. If you now tear up other areas, you're working with a wavy grain pattern and you will have to plane each area separately, with the grain.

A WORD ABOUT SAFETY

The only cause of injuries in your shop is you.

You must be attentive to what you and your tools are doing. Wear ear and eye protection, not just because they reduce eye and ear injuries, but because they reduce distractions. Understand your machinery and the forces it generates. You will notice that some of the photographs in this book show my table saw without its guard in place. This is common practice in all the shops I have visited, a result of the fact that table saw guards prevent several of the operations we often perform. The other guards on my machines stay in place. I value them because they remind me of the dangers involved, rather than suggesting that they are capable of protecting me from harm. Keep your tools in good working order and keep them sharp. Be particularly wary of machines that seem benign, such as the jointer—they can lull you into complacency. If you suspect that a task might be risky on a machine, do it by hand. Hand tools are slower: you make mistakes more slowly and you cut yourself more slowly. Have I made myself clear yet? Okay, just one more.

Machines never make mistakes—only the operator does.

Move Over

DESIGNED BY THOMAS STENDER

This delicate occasional table seems ready to glide across the floor. Its offset top and tapered legs all curving in the same direction propel this design away from its comfortable Shaker heritage.

Materials

$\frac{4}{4}$ cherry

$\frac{8}{4}$ cherry

Supplies

2½" drywall screws

$\frac{3}{16}$" washers

Cutting List

CODE	DESCRIPTION	QTY	MATERIAL	DIMENSIONS
A	Top	1	$\frac{4}{4}$ cherry	19" x 30" x ⅝"
B	Legs	4	$\frac{8}{4}$ cherry	25¼" long
C	Short Aprons	2	$\frac{4}{4}$ cherry	2½" x 12" x ⅞"
D	Long Aprons	2	$\frac{4}{4}$ cherry	2½" x 21" x ⅞"

MAKING THE TOP

1. Begin by flattening and thicknessing enough stock for the top (A). It's finished size will be 19" x 30" x ⅞", so leave enough extra stock for trimming to size. (See Flattening, Thicknessing, and Jointing on page 8 for help.) Lay the planed pieces edge-to-edge so that the grain forms a pleasing pattern. (See Keeping Table Tops Flat on page 9 for advice on arranging the top pieces.)

2. Glue up the top (A). (See Gluing Table Tops on page 10 for help.) Photo 1 shows the top in clamps.

3. Scrape off any excess glue. Square and straighten one edge with the jointer or a jointer plane.

4. Rip the top to slightly over 19" wide and cut the ends square to the 30" final length.

5. Joint the ripped edge smooth. The top (A) is now ready for sanding and finishing. You may do this now, or wait until the rest of the pieces are ready for sanding and finishing. If you sand and finish now, you run a lower risk of carelessly leaving something laying on the top, which will quickly produce a light area on the cherry. Sand all the faces and edges to 220 grit, taking particular care to get all the white marks off the end grain. If you don't know what I mean, start sanding and keep sanding. Round all corners with 220-grit paper after all other sanding is finished. Use your favorite clear finish and please read Burnished Oil Finish on page 20 if you haven't done so already.

MAKING THE LEGS

1. To make the legs (B), you must make a pattern for their shape. Refer to figure 1 and to Fair Curves and Patterns on page 12 to draw and cut the leg pattern from matte board or good-quality ⅛" or ¼" plywood. Make sure to cut your pattern material to 25¼" long, with both ends square to a straight edge before you start drawing the shape.

Photo 1

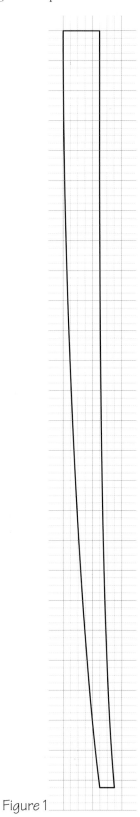

Figure 1

2. Begin the legs (B) themselves by flattening and thicknessing a piece of ¾ cherry at least 26" long to at least 1¾" thick. It will be most efficient to begin with a plank at least 6" wide, so that all four legs can be cut from the same piece.

3. Joint one edge straight and square. Cut one end square, measure and mark 25¼", and cut to length.

4. The sides of the tops of the legs, where they meet the aprons, should be cut on the table saw. This is done with the leg blank held vertically on a table saw. Use a rip blade if you have one, or use a combination blade. Raise the saw blade to 2¾" above the table. Refer to photo 2. The first cut is made against the rip fence. If your rip fence is not 3" tall, you should clamp a straight plank, at least 3" wide, on edge against the fence. This plank must be long enough to allow at least 7" of free space both in front of and behind the blade. Set the rip fence 1¼" from the near side of the blade. Remember to measure from a tooth set toward the fence. Stand the blank for the legs on end, upside down, with the good face against the fence. Turn the saw on and push the blank smoothly and firmly through the blade area, keeping it tight against the fence.

5. To cut the upper ends of the individual legs, use the miter gauge in combination with either a drop stop or the rip fence to make four cuts, 1¼" apart, through the thickness of the plank. Refer to photo 3. Remember to allow for the saw kerf. You will have to flip the plank or move the miter gauge to the other side of the blade to complete all the cuts (see photos 4 and 5). Looking at the top end of the leg blank, you now have four 1¼" squares with ⅛" kerfs between them.

Photo 3

Photo 4

Photo 5

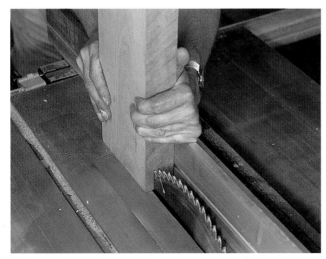

Photo 2

6. Lay the blank on your bench with its good face up. Measuring from the edge with a 1¼" leg top, mark the other (leg bottom) end at 1¾", 3⅛", 4½", and 5⅞". See figure 2. Lay the leg pattern on the blank, with its top end even with the 1¼" area and the bottom point at the appropriate mark. Trace the pattern with a sharp pencil. Repeat for the other three legs.

7. Band saw to the traced lines, as shown in photos 6, 7, and 8. Begin cutting at the top end of each line, being careful not to cut into the sawn faces. The width of the pencil line will allow enough room to smooth back to the pattern dimension.

8. Lay the pattern on the concave side of each leg, top end aligned with the 1¼" area and bottom point 1¾" from the "good" edge. Use a spring clamp or two to hold the pattern in place. Trace the pattern with a sharp pencil. Band saw to the lines as before.

9. With the top end of each leg held by a bench vise, use a low-angle block plane and a spokeshave to smooth the band-sawn areas of the legs. Keep the sides square to each other and run your hand along the surface often to make sure that the curve is fair. (Remember: a fair curve is one without humps or hollows.) Sight along each long corner line also. This will reveal any unfairness immediately. Avoid running into the table-sawn areas at the top of the leg, and try to make the curve of the leg flow smoothly into the straight portion at the top. Don't attempt to smooth the band-sawn surfaces with a power sander of any sort. You won't be able to achieve a fair curve on the concave sides of the legs. If you don't believe me, try it, and then begin the legs again with a fresh piece of cherry.

10. The legs should now be pretty smooth, very fair, and have sharp corners where the sides meet. Sand the legs smooth, beginning with 100- or 120-grit paper and moving through the grits to 220. Use a sanding block, and keep the sides of the legs flat crosswise and the curves fair. When the sides are ready for finish, use 220-grit paper without a block to round the corners slightly. Make sure those legs are really smooth and really fair before you take a break. Believe it or not, the table is almost complete.

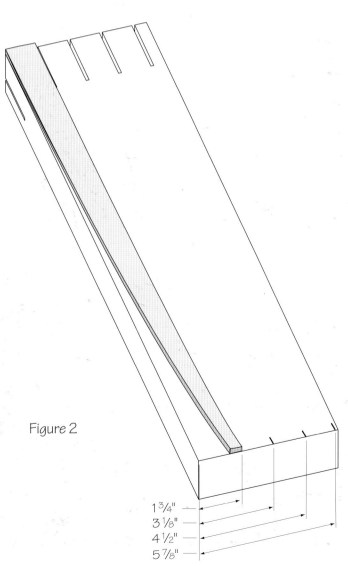

Figure 2

1 ¾"
3 ⅛"
4 ½"
5 ⅞"

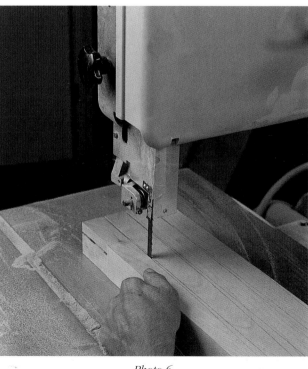

Photo 6

MAKING THE APRONS

1. Choose ¾ stock for the aprons. Flatten it, thickness it to ⅞" or so, joint one edge, and rip it to 2½" wide. Cut two short aprons (C) 12" long and two long aprons (D) 21" long. Photos 9 and 10 show a short apron being cut using a drop stop.

2. Find and mark the better face and the better edge of each apron. These will be the outside face and bottom edge of the aprons when they are assembled. On the bottom edge of each apron (C and D), mark a point 1½" from each end. On the bottom edge of each long apron (D), mark the center lengthwise.

3. The table top (A) will be attached to the aprons (C and D) with 2½" drywall screws driven through ¾6" holes to allow the top to expand and contract. The screw heads are retained by ¾6" washers in ⅝6" countersunk holes. Using a drill press or a hand drill with a ⅝6" bit, drill a hole ½" deep into the bottom edges of the aprons, centered at each mark you made in step 2.

4. Using a ¾6" bit, drill from the center of each countersunk hole through the other (top) edge. Push a 2½" screw with a washer through these holes to make sure that the point of the screw protrudes ½" on the top of the apron. If it protrudes less than ½", you must drill the countersink deeper. If it protrudes more than ½", you must try again with a second washer on the screw.

Photo 7

Photo 9

Photo 8

Photo 10

CUTTING THE JOINTS AND ASSEMBLING THE TABLE

1. Now you must determine the arrangement of the legs. Hold the four legs (B) together at their tops so that their curves run in the same diagonal direction. If the inside faces of the legs in the top 2½" fit together snugly, you will likely be able to make snug joints with the aprons (C and D). If they don't match closely, try rearranging the legs to get a better fit. When you're satisfied with the arrangement, draw a square on the top end grain of the leg bundle so that a segment of the square points to each face that will join a apron. A corner of the square will be near the center of each leg.

2. The legs (B) and aprons (C and D) are joined with biscuits. See Biscuit Joinery on page 16 to review. Use the "1" setting on your machine with #10 biscuits. The aprons (C and D) are set back from the outside surfaces of the legs by ⅛", so there will be different fence settings for the legs and the aprons. One biscuit per joint is probably sufficient, but I generally use two biscuits per joint to make it stronger and because it's so easy to add a second one. Set the fence of your biscuit joiner to ¼". With the good (outside) face against the fence, cut a centered slot into both ends of all four aprons, as shown in photo 11. Be careful to cut accurately because there is very little space between the ends of the slots and the top and bottom edges of the aprons.

3. Set the fence of your biscuit joiner to ⅝". With the good face against the fence, cut a second centered slot into both ends of all four aprons.

4. Set the fence of your biscuit joiner to ⅜" for the first slots in the legs. The slots will be centered 1¼" below the tops of the legs. If you are using the biscuit joiner right side up, mark this point at the corner between each outside face and its adjacent face to be joined. If you are using the biscuit joiner upside down in a vise, use the end of one of the aprons, centered on the cutter, to mark its two edges on the base of the joiner. You will use each of these marks to cut one slot in each leg, as shown in photo 12.

5. With the outside face of each leg (B) against the fence, and the joint face toward the cutter, aligned carefully, cut the outer slots into the joint faces of the legs. You will have to flip each leg lengthwise to cut the slot in the second joint face.

6. Set the fence of your biscuit joiner to ¾" for the inner slots in the legs. Cut these slots as before.

7. Sand both faces and the bottom edge of each apron (C and D) to 220 grit. Round both corners adjacent to the bottom edges with 220 grit paper. You may finish all the pieces of the table now or wait until the legs and aprons are assembled. Finishing the pieces before assembly makes it easier to wipe (or peel) off excess glue because it won't be absorbed into the wood. See Burnished Oil Finish on page 20.

8. Assemble the legs (B) and aprons (C and D) upside down on a smooth, flat surface protected by plastic or paper. Lay out all the base pieces in their relative positions, making sure that the curves of the legs all go in the same diagonal direction. Are the

Photo 11

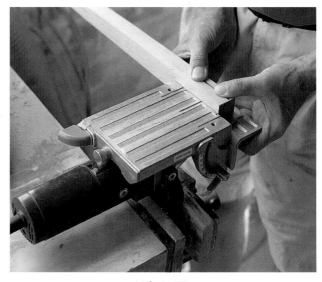

Photo 12

short aprons (C) opposite each other, standing on their top edges, with their good sides outward? Same with the long aprons (D)? I thought so. Fetch your glue bottle and get out more than enough #10 biscuits. Make sure that four clamps with pads are ready to hand. You need one clamp for each side of the base. A cloth or piece of rubber near the edge of your work table will come in very handy to protect the legs as you push the pieces together.

9. Distribute a small amount of yellow glue in all four slots in one leg, and quickly press four biscuits into position. Repeat on the other three legs.

10. Distribute a small amount of yellow glue in all four slots in one long apron (D), and quickly push its two legs into position, with the top edge of the apron flush with the tops of the legs. Repeat immediately with the other long apron (D) and its legs. Don't stop to admire your work.

11. Glue the slots in the same end of both of the short aprons (C) and push them against their legs. Place the assembly so far on your padded area with the free ends of the short aprons pointing up. Glue the last four slots and press the remaining legs (with their long apron) into position.

12. Place the assembled base upside down, check that the top surfaces (now against the work surface) look flush, and begin clamping. Apply clamps to opposite sides first, then add the cross clamps. Make sure that the clamps exert pressure in line with the centers of the apron ends. Use a ruler to check the diagonals to make sure the assembly is square. If it isn't, try to correct the condition by changing the clamping pressure or by moving the clamp faces slightly. Check every joint to make sure that it's tight. Are the top edges of all the aprons and the tops of all the legs still touching the work surface?

Thomas Stender, *Swept Away*, 1987; curly cherry; 30" x 19" x 26"; photo by K. C. Kratt. This table provided inspiration for the Move Over project.

13. Okay, breathe. Then wipe off any visible glue.

14. If you've left any pieces unfinished, you must completely finish them now. (If you had done this when I told you to, you would be ready to assemble your table right now.)

15. Place the table top (A) face down on a padded surface. Place the leg assembly top down on the table top and position it so that the convex surfaces of three legs are 1" from the edges of the top. Refer to figure 3.

16. Put washers on ten 2½" drywall screws. If you found that you needed extra washers on any screws

in step 4 of Making the Aprons, make sure that you add them now and put those screws in the correct holes. With all the screws in their holes, lift the leg assembly to make sure that no screw looks like it will go through the top. Then put the assembly back in its proper position on the top.

17. Using a power driver with the clutch set for light pressure, drive the screws. Press down hard to get the screws to self-thread quickly. Check for proper position after each of the first several screws. Increase the clutch pressure a little if necessary to tighten the screw heads against their washers. Turn the table right side up and admire your work.

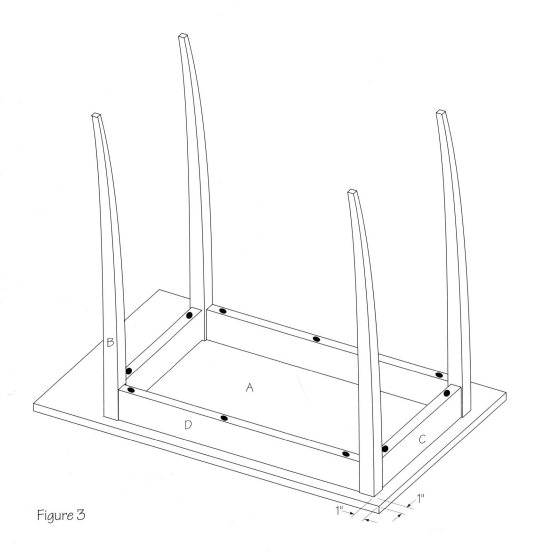

Figure 3

Centered Square Table

DESIGNED BY RON TRUMBLE

"Simple design is the most difficult to design," says Ron Trumble of this table, in which lines and a square suggest a restrained ornamentalism. A bit "like doing jewelry in furniture," the inlays will challenge any woodworker, but the result certainly justifies our efforts. By the way, Trumble constructs this table in three hours.

Materials

Black-dyed veneer

Ebony

¾" plywood veneered in birdseye maple

¼ cherry

¼ maple

⅝ cherry

Supplies

#20 biscuits

2" x 4½" corner brackets with screws

#6 x 1½" pan head screws

Cutting List

CODE	DESCRIPTION	QTY	MATERIAL	DIMENSIONS
A	Top Panel	1	plywood with birdseye maple veneer	¾" x 14" x 14"
B	Black Lines	4	black-dyed veneer	doubled x ⅛" x 10"
C	Center Square	1	ebony	¼" x ¼" x ½"
D	Border Stripes	4	ebony	⅛" x ⅛" x 14"
E	Top Borders	4	cherry	¾" x 3" x 20"
F	Legs	4	cherry	1" x 2⅞" x 19¼"
G	Aprons	4	maple	¾" x 3" x 14"

INLAYING THE TOP PANEL

1. Veneer a piece of high-quality ¾" plywood larger than 14" square with birdseye maple veneer. (See Simple Veneering on page 18 for help.) Trim the veneered plywood to 14" square for the top panel (A) by cutting two adjacent sides absolutely square. Then use the rip fence set at 14" from the blade to cut the other two sides.

2. Cut two strips of black-dyed veneer, 1" x 11", and glue them together. Clamp them between boards protected by sheets of plastic film.

3. Use a veneer saw to cut four ⅛"-wide strips from the doubled veneer.

4. Your next task has "risk" written all over it. (Or it would if there were room, which is precisely the problem.) You must cut grooves diagonally across the top panel into which the doubled veneer will fit.

Snugly. First find a saw with a convex-shaped blade which produces a kerf about 1/20" wide. The veneer saw may work, or a thin Japanese flooring saw. If your saw kerf is slightly narrow, try block-sanding the doubled veneer a little bit, but don't round the strip. Clamp a straight-edged board across the top panel, offset from the corners only enough to put the center of the kerf at the corner point. Notice photo 1, which shows me holding a ruler with one hand, like a fool. Hold the blade of the saw against the straightedge with the fingers of one hand while sawing 1/16"-3/32" deep from corner to corner. Start breathing again, then cut the other diagonal.

5. Apply glue to a groove, from the center to a corner, with a very thin sliver of wood. Start one doubled

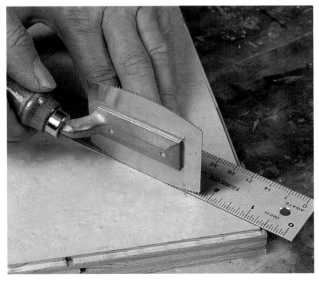

Photo 1

Photo 2

veneer strip where the grooves cross, and gently tap it into place, working toward the corner (see photo 2). Insert the other lines in the same way. Keep the beginning ends within ⅛" of the center cross.

6. When the glue has cured, saw the ends of the strips flush with the edge of the panel. Scrape the veneer flush with the surface of the panel using a cabinet scraper, properly sharpened and burnished. If you sand the dyed veneer, you must take great care to blow the black dust out of the tiny pores in the birdseye maple.

Photo 3

Photo 4

7. To start the ¼"-square hole in the center of the panel, drill ⅛" deep with a ⁷⁄₃₂" bit. Try the bit on a scrap to see if it's likely to tear up the surrounding surface. If you don't have a suitable bit, you're better off cutting the recess with a chisel alone. A ¼" mortise chisel is best for this job. Mark the square with a thin-bladed craft knife. Make sure that the square isn't smaller than your chisel is wide. On successive passes with the knife, cut through the veneer. Sharpen your chisel. Begin cutting a little back from the line, so that the bevel of the chisel doesn't force the chisel outward, crushing wood past the line. Work patiently, clearing the middle of the hole as you go deeper. Try to avoid the "cave in" visible in photo 3, which allowed a piece of veneer to break away. The resulting space had to be filled in later.

8. Make the center square (C) from a small strip of ebony. It should be exactly the same size as the square hole, so exactly that it seems a bit oversize. Chamfer the corners on one end. Apply five-minute epoxy to the hole, and tap the square into place (see photo 4). Let the glue cure thoroughly.

9. Cut off the excess square with a Japanese saw, and carefully pare the stub flush with the veneered surface (see photo 5).

10. Put a large bearing on your router's rabbet bit, and cut a ⅛" x ⅛" rabbet around the top edge of the top panel.

11. Mill the border stripes (D) from ebony, leaving them slightly larger than the dimensions of the rabbet. Cut one end of each stripe square. Apply five-minute epoxy to the rabbet on one side of the panel. Hold a

Photo 5

piece of border stripe in an adjacent rabbet, and butt the square end of a border stripe against it in the glued rabbet. Hold the border stripe in place with good-quality plastic masking tape or artists' tape, as shown in photo 6.

12. Apply glue to the rabbet next to the long end of the first stripe. Butt the next border stripe against the first, and tape it down. Apply the other stripes in the same way.

13. Saw off the ends of the border stripes. Scrape them flush with the veneered surface and with the edges of the top panel. Do not round them over or scrape past flush.

COMPLETING THE TABLE TOP

1. Flatten, thickness, and joint one edge of cherry boards for the top borders (E). (See Flattening, Thicknessing, and Jointing on page 8 for a refresher course). You may as well prepare the stock for the aprons (G), since their thicknesses and widths are the same as those of the borders. Rip the material to just over 3", and clean up the new edge with one pass over the jointer.

2. Miter the ends of the top borders very carefully, matching each border to a particular side of the top panel and marking the border and the side. Before cutting any aprons to length, make sure that you're cutting 45° accurately by cutting a miter on one end each of two pieces of border. Hold these against a corner of the top panel to look for gaps in the miter joint. Adjust your setup as necessary, and try again. When your angles are accurate, mark and cut the borders to length. If you happen to cut one short,

remember that jointing its inside edge will effectively lengthen that edge, giving you another chance.

3. With the borders laid out around the panel, mark across the joints for the biscuit jointer (see Biscuit Joinery on page 16 for help). Mark the middle of each miter joint, and mark 3" in from each panel corner along the edge joints. Use the biscuit jointer base flat on your bench, and cut slots for #20 biscuits at every mark (see photo 7).

4. Make sure you have clamps, pads, biscuits, glue, and a pure heart before you begin assembling the top. You must work quickly and accurately throughout this process. Lay out the top panel and the top borders in their relative positions. Glue and push biscuits into all the slots in the top panel first. Then glue and biscuit the left end of each border (you decide which is which). Glue the slots and edges of each border in turn and push it into place. Make sure to get each one positioned accurately as you go—those biscuits puff up quickly. Because of that, Ron Trumble suggests positioning two opposite aprons first, clamping them, and then pushing the other two into place. After you clamp across the top, check for flatness with a straightedge across all the joints. Adjust the clamp positions to correct any misalignment.

5. Scrape off excess glue, and sand the completed top to 220 grit or finer. You will, of course, avoid sanding through the veneer. Blow compressed air and/or vacuum to clean every bit of black dust from the birdseye veneer. Ease the corners around the edge.

Photo 6

Photo 7

MAKING THE LEGS AND APRONS

1. Flatten, thickness, and joint one edge of two boards at least 4" wide for the legs (F). Rip them to just over 4", and joint the ripped edge. Cut the boards square to 19¼" long, using a drop stop (see Drop Stops, Jigs, and Fixtures on page 12).

2. On each board, measure and mark along the end a point ¹¹⁄₁₆" from an edge. On the opposite end, mark at ¹¹⁄₁₆" from the other edge, as shown in figure 1. Draw a straight line between the points. Band saw down the center of that line, wavering not a bit. Joint to clean up the saw marks.

3. Set the rip fence on your table saw to 3" to rip off the top corner of each leg. Adjust the fence until the vertical edge is 2½" long (see figure 2).

4. Stand a leg on its outer (straight) edge. Use two apron pieces as spacers under your biscuit jointer to cut a #10 slot, centered 1½" from the top end, into the side of the leg. (See photo 8, in which the aprons have already been mitered.) Cut another slot on the other side of the leg, and cut two slots in each of the other legs.

5. Use a ½"-radius round-over router bit to shape the outside edge of each leg (see photo 9). This is easiest if you use a split fence on a router table and hold the leg with its outside edge down on the table.

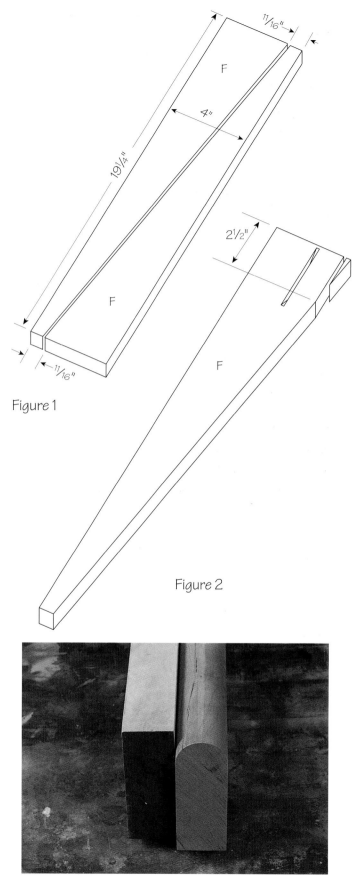

Figure 1

Figure 2

Photo 8

Photo 9

6. With the table saw blade tilted 45°, use the miter gauge with a drop stop to cut miters across the thickness of each apron, leaving the aprons 14" long. Keep or make mitered scraps at least 6" long to test the slots for the corner brackets.

7. Using the miter fence on your biscuit jointer, cut #10 slots, centered ⁵⁄₁₆" from the inside corner of the miter and centered widthwise on the apron, into the mitered ends of the aprons. Cut similar slots in the mitered ends of the test pieces you made in the previous step.

8. Mark the inside face of each apron at points 3" in from the miters and 1¼" from the top edge. Tilt the table on your drill press 20°, and attach a fence which will hold the aprons while you drill from the marked points through the top edge. Start each hole

Photo 10

with a ⅜" forstner bit, and stop 1" from the top edge, at a point where you have a shoulder for the screw head to bear against (see photo 10). From the center of that hole, drill through the top edge with a bit sized to the outside diameter of your screw threads (⁹⁄₆₄" for a #6 screw).

9. The corner brackets for the aprons require saw kerfs, positioned very accurately, on the inside faces of the aprons. Lower the blade on your table saw until it cuts only deep enough to accommodate the flanges on your corner brackets. Set the rip fence on the opposite side of the blade from the miter gauge. With the mitered end of your test pieces against the rip fence, begin cutting kerf slots across their inside faces a little farther out than you think they should be. Try the fit with the test pieces, a leg, and a bracket. Move the rip fence gradually closer to the blade until the bracket fits perfectly with the test pieces and the leg. Then cut slots in the aprons themselves (see photo 11).

10. Assemble the legs and aprons, with their biscuits, upside down on a flat surface, holding it all together with a band clamp. With the brackets in place, drill pilot holes for their screws into the aprons. Mark the inside edge of each leg for its bracket screw (see photo 12). When you've disassembled the base, drill pilot holes in the legs for #10 screws.

11. Sand the aprons and legs to 220 grit, and ease the long-grain corners. Ron Trumble finishes this table with clear lacquer, a good choice because it preserves the sharp contrast between the colors of the top.

Photo 11

Photo 12

12. Assemble the table upside down on a padded surface. Use #10 x 3" screws with fender washers to attach the brackets to the legs. Center the base on the top, and mark pilot holes with a finishing nail run through the slanted holes in the aprons. Drill ³⁄₃₂" pilot holes only ¼" to ³⁄₈" deep. Use #6 x 1½" pan head screws to fasten the aprons to the top.

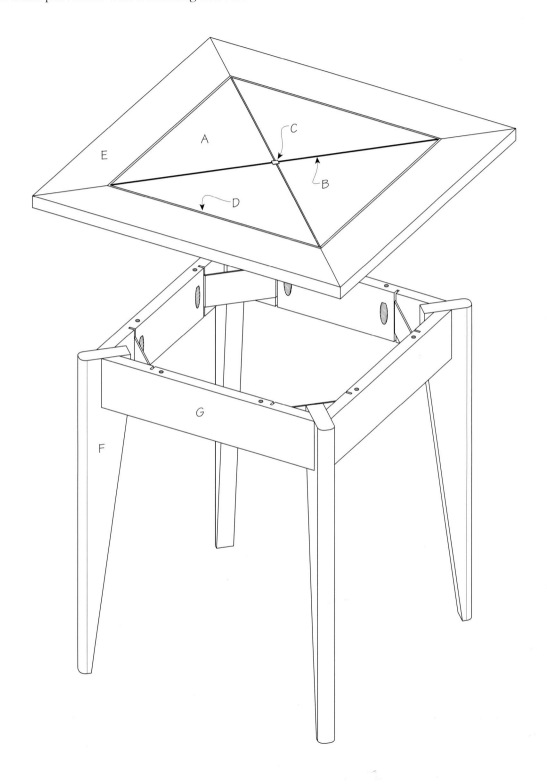

Plant Stand

DESIGNED BY RICHARD JUDD

The legs of this stand derive visual lift from their concave outer edges. They promise to push skyward any plant lucky enough to sit on the top shelf. Make this table in a weekend and enjoy it for years.

Materials

¼ **wenge**

¼ **birdseye maple or padauk**

Supplies

#10 x 1½" pan head tapping screws

Cutting List

CODE	DESCRIPTION	QTY	MATERIAL	DIMENSIONS
A	Legs	4	wenge	2 pcs. ¾" x 3½"+ x 27"
B	Shelves	2	birdseye maple	¾" x 8" x 8"

MAKING THE LEGS

1. Use one board 7½" wide or two narrower pieces. Flatten, thickness, and joint one edge of wenge stock for the legs. (See Flattening, Thicknessing, and Jointing on page 8 to review this process.) Rip two 3½"-wide (or wider) pieces. Joint the ripped edges, then cut them to length.

2. You will saw two legs from each 3½" piece, as shown in figure 1. Using figure 2 as a guide, make a leg pattern from matte board or thin plywood. (See Fair Curves and Patterns on page 12 for useful tips.)

3. Align the ends and the straight edge of the pattern with the ends and one edge of a piece of leg stock. Trace the pattern. Turn the pattern end-for-end, align it, and trace it again.

4. Band saw the legs to the line or barely outside it. Clean up the saw marks with a spokeshave held diagonally to the work. Try for nice, fair curves without any humps or hollows.

5. With a ¾" dado head mounted ¼" high in the table saw, set your rip fence 4" from the near side of the blade. Cut the dadoes for the bottom shelf through the straight edges near the wider end of the legs. Cut all four legs at once to minimize tear-out at the end of the cut.

6. Set the rip fence to 1", turn the legs around, and cut the dado for the top shelf.

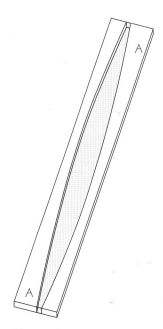

Figure 1

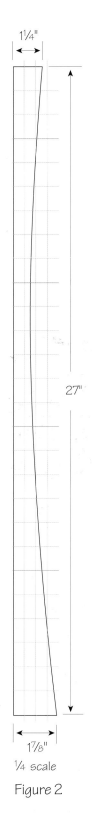

1¼"

27"

1⅞"

¼ scale

Figure 2

7. From the center of each dado, square around to mark the position of the screw holes on the curved edges of the legs. Use a center punch to mark the centerline, thicknesswise, at each mark and to provide a starting point for your drill bit. On the drill press, bore ⅜" countersink holes to ¾" from the straight edge of each leg at each mark. Then drill an ¹¹⁄₆₄" hole from the center of the countersink to the center of the dado.

8. While you're at the drill press, cut at least eight plugs from maple or another wood with a color that contrasts with that of the legs. Use a four-pronged plug cutter for best results.

9. With a ball-bearing 45° bevel-cutting bit in your router, and the router mounted in a router table, cut a ⅛" bevel on all the corners of the legs, except those in the dado. Be careful to avoid dipping into the dado areas. Then sand the legs to 220 grit, keeping the bevels crisp. Leave the router set up, because the shelves need bevels, too.

MAKING THE SHELVES AND FINISHING THE TABLE

1. Prepare figured maple or padauk stock for the shelves. As you thickness it, compare the board to the dadoes in the legs. Stop planing when the thickness of the shelf stock is at the point of sliding into the dado. Joint one edge and cut one end square. Check the angle to make sure it's square. Set the rip fence on the table saw to 8" and make two more cross-grain cuts (with the newly cut end grain against the rip fence), then rip the two shelves square.

2. Use the 45° cutter in the router table to bevel the corners around the top and bottom faces of the shelves.

Photo 1

Photo 2

3. Sand the shelves to 220 grit on all six surfaces. Sand the bevels carefully to keep them sharp. Check the thickness of the shelves with the leg dadoes as you sand. The shelves must slide into the dadoes, but they shouldn't be loose (photo 1).

4. Set the miter gauge on the table saw to 45° with the blade end of the fence forward. Use a drop stop to set the length of the corners to be cut from the shelves. Begin by cutting a very small piece from the corner of one shelf. Compare the corner with the thickness of a leg, move the drop stop slightly, and cut again. The length of the bevel on the corners of the shelves should be slightly less than the thickness of the legs, so that the sides of the shelves won't end outside the dado. Refer to photo 2, which shows the proper relationship.

5. Mark the joint areas of the legs and shelves with numbers or letters so you know how they go together after finishing. The grain in the two shelves should run in the same direction. Clamp a shelf in your bench vise with one of its corners up. Slide the appropriate dado onto the shelf, and center it over the corner. Drill a ⅛" pilot hole at least 1" deep into the shelf, centered in the clearance hole in the leg. Repeat this process with every other joint.

6. Use #10 x 1½" pan head tapping screws to assemble the table. If one of the screws strips out, replace it with a 1¾" screw.

7. Dip each plug in a puddle of woodworking glue and tap it into a countersink with a tack hammer. Be sure to leave some plug sticking out. When the glue has set, pare off the excess plug with a sharp chisel. Don't try to whack it off with one mighty blow because you risk splitting the grain below the surface of the leg. Sand the plug areas with 220 grit.

8. Finish the table with a burnished oil finish (see page 20) or another clear finish. Richard Judd lacquers his tables.

Figure 3

43

Hall Table

DESIGNED BY MARK C. TAYLOR

Materials

¼ maple

¼ poplar

⅘ poplar

Supplies

Table top fasteners and screws

Corner brackets and screws

Attractive and functional behind a sofa or in a hallway, this table features a Shaker-like simplicity that will complement many interiors. For the top, use that special board you've been saving.

Cutting List

CODE	DESCRIPTION	QTY	MATERIAL	DIMENSIONS
A	Top	1	maple	¾" x 10½" x 54"
B	Legs	4	poplar or maple	1½" x 1½" x 28¼"
C	Long Aprons	2	poplar or maple	¾" x 2½" x 39"
D	Short Aprons	2	poplar or maple	¾" x 2½" x 6½"

MAKING THE TOP

1. Flatten, thickness, and joint one edge of a pretty piece of maple for the table top (A). (See Flattening, Thicknessing, and Jointing on page 8 for help.) Rip it to slightly over 10½" wide, and lightly joint the ripped edge. Cut the ends to produce a top 54" long.

2. To make the molded edge you will need a 1" round-over router bit (or an equivalent shaper cutter) and a router table with a split fence. You need a substantial router for this operation. Set the fence ⅛" ahead of the ball bearing on the bit and set the square corner of the bit 1⁄16" above the table. Begin with the end grain and proceed to cut around the top with the good face down on the router table. Then move the fence back to 1⁄16" ahead of the ball bearing for the final cut. This produces a 15⁄16"-wide molding. If you don't have a router table, it would be possible to clamp a board under the top, protruding ⅛" and then 1⁄16", for the ball bearing to ride against on each edge of the top.

3. Sand the top to 220 grit, taking care to preserve the crispness of the molded corner of the top surface. The molded end grain will take extra care and time. You'll

know you're finished when the grain is clear and no white areas remain. Ease the bottom corners all around.

4. Finish the top with the burnished oil finish described on page 20, or with a clear finish of your choice.

MAKING THE LEGS

1. Prepare 1½" square poplar or maple stock for the legs (B). Cut the ends to produce 28¼"-long pieces.

2. The two inside faces of the legs are tapered to ¾" square at the bottom. The outside faces remain straight. The taper begins 2¾" from the top of the leg. You may wish to make a taper jig as illustrated on page 80 to cut the legs with a ripping blade on the table saw. You could also draw the lines on each leg, cut them slightly outside the line with a band saw, and clean the sawn faces on the jointer. There are only four legs, so both methods would take about the same time.

3. Chamfer the inside corner at the top of each leg about ¼" wide to make the pilot hole for the bracket

screw easier to start. (That is, if you're using brackets. See Joinery Options below.)

4. Sand the legs to 220, easing the corners slightly, and taking care to keep the inside faces at the tops of the legs flat and square.

JOINERY OPTIONS

Mark Taylor uses corner brackets to hold the legs and aprons together and table top fasteners to hold the aprons to the top. This is a very direct method of joinery and facilitates shipping his tables. You may choose to join the legs to the aprons with biscuits (see Biscuit Joinery on page 16) and/or fasten the aprons to the top with screws in oversize holes. This

method is used for Move Over. Refer to pages 29-32 for a description of the procedure. For this Hall Table, use #10 biscuits and set the aprons in ¼" from the outside faces of the legs.

MAKING THE APRONS AND ASSEMBLING THE TABLE

1. Prepare maple or poplar stock ¾" thick and 2½" wide for the long and short aprons (C and D). Cut the long aprons to 39" and the short aprons to 6½".

2. Cut slots for the six table top fasteners on the inside faces of the long aprons. You may cut six slots with a biscuit joiner, or you may cut one long, ¼"-deep slot with the table saw. In either case, the slot must begin slightly more than the depth of the fastener from the top edge of the apron. Usually this distance is ⅜", but check your fasteners before cutting the slots. If you use a biscuit joiner, center one slot lengthwise on each long apron and cut the others about 5" from the ends of the aprons (see figure 1).

Photo 1

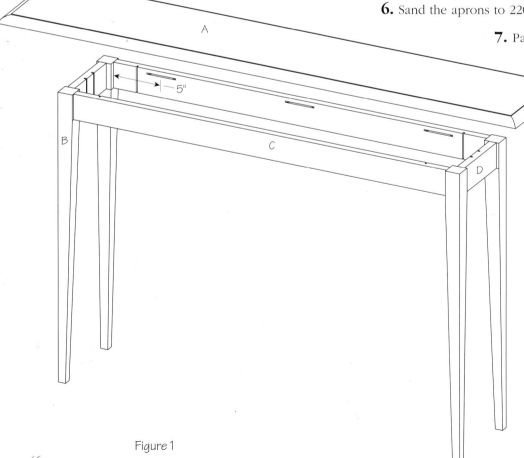

Figure 1

3. The corner brackets require vertical slots on the inside faces of the long and short aprons. Stand a leg upside down on a flat surface, and butt a long and a short apron up to the inside faces of the leg. The outside faces of the leg should protrude ¼" from the outside faces of the aprons. Hold one of your brackets on top of the aprons so that its flanges are equidistant from the leg. Mark the aprons at the flanges.

4. With the table saw blade set ¼" high (or enough to accommodate the flanges on your brackets), set the rip fence a little farther from the blade than the distance from your marks to the ends of the aprons. You will want to test this distance on scraps before cutting slots in your aprons. Use the miter gauge to maintain control of the apron, and place the end of the apron against the rip fence as you make your cut. Cut slots in two scraps. Test the rip fence setting by assembling the scraps with the leg and the bracket. You can keep using the same scraps to gradually arrive at a perfect fit. Then cut bracket slots in each end of all the aprons.

5. Assemble the legs, aprons, and brackets upside down on a flat surface. Mark the positions of all screw holes in the legs and aprons. Drill appropriate pilot holes at all those marks.

6. Sand the aprons to 220, easing the bottom corners.

7. Paint the legs and the aprons with black lacquer or send them out to be professionally finished.

8. Assemble the legs, aprons, and brackets upside down on a flat surface. Drive all necessary screws to attach the brackets to the aprons and to pull the legs into place.

9. Place the top (A) upside down on a padded surface. Position the base assembly upside down on the top, centering it both ways. Drill pilot holes for the table top fastener screws and drive them snug. There! You're done already.

Low Fat Table

DESIGNED BY THOMAS STENDER

Perfect for a low sofa, or to suggest a Japanese atmosphere in an open room, Low Fat was inspired by its innovative construction method. We do not often get an opportunity to work with such large masses in wood. What an advantage to be able to lift the table with one hand!

Materials

¼" plywood, cherry-veneered

2" polystyrene foam insulation

⅜" x ⅜" cherry strips

Supplies

4 mil. or thicker polyethylene film

Structural epoxy

Cutting List

CODE	DESCRIPTION	QTY	MATERIAL	DIMENSIONS
A	Top Fill	2	polystyrene foam	2" x 20" x 42"
B	Top Panel	1	cherry-veneered plywood	¼" x 20" x 42"
C	Bottom Panel	1	lauan plywood	¼" x 20" x 42"
D	Long Side Panel	2	cherry-veneered plywood	¼" x 3⅞" x 42"
E	Short Side Panel	2	cherry-veneered plywood	¼" x 3⅞" x 19⅞"
F	Long strips	4	cherry	⅜" x ⅜" x 42½"
G	Short strips	4	cherry	⅜" x ⅜" x 20½"
H	Vertical strips	4	cherry	⅜" x ⅜" x 4½"
I	Leg fill	2	polystyrene foam	2" x 14" x 14"
J	Wide leg panel	2	cherry-veneered plywood	¼" x 14" x 14"
K	Narrow leg panel	2	cherry-veneered plywood	¼" x 3⅞" x 14"
L	Leg strips	4	cherry	⅜" x ⅜" x 14"

Photo 1

Photo 2

LAMINATING THE TOP AND LEGS

You may either purchase ¼" plywood veneered with cherry, or veneer your own plywood. Consult a book or article about veneering if you haven't made large panels before. If you want your table to last, don't use contact cement to veneer the panels. Instead, use woodworking glue of some sort in a press.

1. Cut the pieces of top fill (A) and leg fill (I) on the table saw, making sure to cut the pieces for each exactly the same size.

2. Cut the top panel (B), bottom panel (C), and the wide leg panels (J) to size. While you're at it, cut pieces of scrap plywood for pressure blocks the same sizes as the panels.

3. Stack the panels and fill in the order in which they will be glued. For instance, on top of a scrap panel

for the table top, placed good side up, lay a larger piece of plastic film, then the top panel (B), good side down, two pieces of top fill (A), the bottom panel (C), good side up, another sheet of plastic, and a second scrap panel.

4. Gather your epoxy tools: plastic paint tray, small roller frame, short foam roller cover, plastic mixing cup, mixing stick. Put on disposable rubber gloves and mix some epoxy. If you work quickly, you should be able to mix enough for the whole table at once. Add some microfibers or other filler to keep the epoxy from completely soaking into the wood and foam. Pour the epoxy into your tray. Turn over the scrap panel, plastic sheet, and bottom panel. Then begin spreading epoxy on both surfaces of every joint to be glued, as shown in photos 1 and 2. Continue spreading the glue on the wide leg panels (J) and the leg fill (I) before putting pressure on the sandwiches.

5. Of course you know where in your shop you have large enough flat areas to press the top sandwich and the leg sandwich. Of course you do. So find them quickly right now. And you will have found enough weights to put even pressure on the sandwiches. So figure that out, too. Don't worry: the epoxy doesn't set up that fast. You have at least 14½ minutes from right now. Consult photos 3 and 4 for some ideas on weighting—boxes of books and hydraulic jacks are shown. My calculations show that I had 12 tons of

Photo 3

Photo 4

weight on the leg sandwich. Make sure you keep the stacks lined up exactly. That will save a lot of fooling around later.

6. When the glue has cured, make sure that the two fill pieces in each sandwich are still aligned. You must make all sides of the top sandwich flat, and you must make both long sides of the leg sandwich flat, before proceeding. Cut the long side panels (D), short side panels (E), and narrow leg panels (K) to size.

7. Prepare a suitable clamping strategy for the long side panels (D). Then mix epoxy as before, spread it on all joint surfaces, and clamp up. Don't forget to add plastic sheets between the side panels and your back-up panels or clamps. See that the panels are laying flat against the foam. (See photo 5.)

8. When the glue has cured, glue the short side panels (E) to the ends of the top and the narrow leg panels (K) to the sides of the leg sandwich.

Photo 5

TRIMMING THE CORNERS AND COMPLETING THE TABLE

1. Clean up any cured glue from the faces of the panels. With a ball-bearing-guided ⅜" rabbet bit in your router, set ⅜" deep, rout a rabbet on every corner where two panels meet, both on the top and on the leg sandwich.

2. Prepare cherry strips to fill the rabbets you just cut. Leave them slightly oversize. You will need the equivalent of five strips 6' long.

3. Because they are easiest, glue in the leg strips (L) first. Cut the strips to length. You may use yellow woodworking glue for these strips because you will be gluing to the edges of the plywood. Apply glue to two adjacent faces of each strip, lay it in place, and hold it there with strips of masking tape stretched around the corner. You can use another kind of tape if the masking tape won't hold your strips. Check them after a few minutes to see that they are still tightly in place.

4. The corner strips around the top should be mitered. Each strip meets two other strips at each end, so each end must be mitered in two directions. Begin with the long strips (F), cutting both miters on one end of each. The squared-across lines where the miters begin must meet each other at their common corner. When that is the case, the slanting corner line

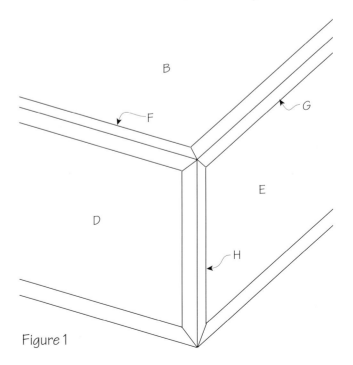

Figure 1

between the two mitered surfaces will extend precisely to the opposite corner of the strip, at the point. Cut double miters on a scrap piece or two to help position the strips and check the miters.

5. Put one long strip in place, checking the position of the mitered end by holding the scrap in each of the adjacent grooves and making sure that the joints are tight. Using a thin-bladed craft knife, mark the ends of the plywood on the other end of the long strip. Use those lines to cut the miters. Check your work with the mitered scraps. If the strip is too short, see if you can use it in another long groove or use it for two short strips (G). If the strip is too long, you're on your own as to a solution. Proceed in the same way to cut the other long strips, marking them to identify their positions.

6. Cut the short strips (G) in the same way you did the long ones. This time, you can tape one long strip in position on a top corner of the table top and another on a bottom corner to help position the short strips for marking. Tape the long strips tightly very near the corners.

7. Tape the long and short strips for the upper corners in position, and remove the long strips from the lower corners. Then mark and cut the vertical strips (H). When all the strips have been cut and checked individually, tape all the strips in position all around the table top to check the miters one last time.

8. Remove one strip at a time to apply glue to the two plywood surfaces in its groove. Then securely tape it back into position. Apply a tiny drop of glue to the miters of strips that have already been glued down.

9. When all the strips have been glued into their rabbets, sand them flush with the surfaces of the top and legs. Then cut the legs to length. Begin by cutting one end using the miter gauge on the table saw. You will need to use two cuts if your saw cannot cut 4½" deep. When that end of the leg sandwich is square both ways, set the rip fence to 6½" to cut the two legs to length.

10. Sand all cherry surfaces to 220 grit, trying to minimize cross-grain scratches, especially on the veneer.

11. Lay the top face down on a padded surface. Place the legs in position, 6" from each end of the top and centered widthwise. Trace around the legs with a pencil to mark their positions. Mix up some epoxy with microfibers or another thickening agent to soft butter consistency, and spread it on the top end of each leg and in the marked areas on the bottom of the table top. Press the legs into position. If the joints look tight and stay that way by themselves, you're done, but you will probably want to weight them to hold their position while the glue cures.

12. Finish the Low Fat Table with the burnished oil finish described on page 20, or with another clear finish.

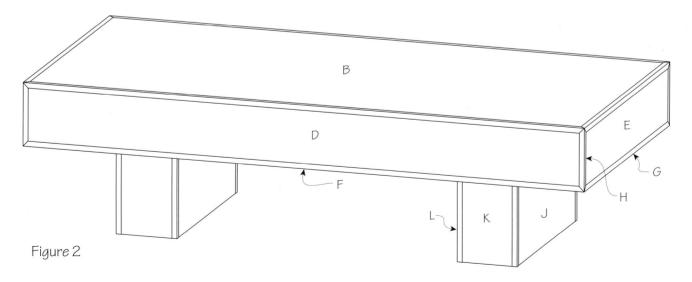

Figure 2

Nested Spindle Tables

DESIGNED BY THOMAS STENDER

Thanks to prefinished balusters, this sweet set of stacking tables goes together easily. The tops of the smaller tables glide into grooves in the next larger legs and aprons, forming one compact unit until you need three tables again.

Materials

- **4/4 cherry**
- **5/4 cherry**
- **White balusters tapered 31"**

Supplies

- **#20 biscuits**
- **2½" screws**
- **3/16" washers**

Cutting List

CODE	DESCRIPTION	QTY	MATERIAL	DIMENSIONS
A	Large Top	1	cherry	¾" x 16¼" x 19½"
B	Medium Top	1	cherry	¾" x 14⅛" x 15¾"
C	Small Top	1	cherry	¾" x 12" x 12"
D	Large Side Aprons	2	cherry	1" x 4½" x 12"
E	Medium Side Aprons	2	cherry	1" x 3¼" x 9⅞"
F	Large Back Apron	1	cherry	1" x 4½" x 15¼"
G	Medium Back Apron	1	cherry	1" x 3¼" x 11½"
H	Small Aprons	2	cherry	1" x 2" x 7¾"
I	Large Legs	4	baluster	23¼" long
J	Medium Legs	4	baluster	21¾" long
K	Small Legs	4	baluster	20½" long

MAKING THE TOPS

1. Notice that the grain of the table tops must run from side to side. Flatten, thickness, joint, and edge glue enough cherry for the three tops (A, B, and C). (Refer to Flattening, Thicknessing, and Jointing on page 8.) Joint one edge of each, then rip to width and cut to length.

2. To make sure that the lip on the edges of the tops is uniformly ¼" thick, the lip should be cut before molding the edge. (You may want to delay this step and the next two until you're ready to cut the grooves in Completing the Aprons and Leg, page 55. That will save unnecessary blade changes.) First, sand the tops

53

to remove glue and to flatten them. Decide which is the top side of each and mark it. With a ⁵⁄₁₆" dado blade in the table saw, set the rip fence to exactly ¼" from the near side of the blade. Stand each top on edge, with its top face tight against the fence, and cut the lip all the way around. (See photo 1.) While you're there, move the fence ¼" farther from the blade and make another pass around the top to remove more waste. (See photo 2.)

3. Use a ½" radius core box bit in your table-mounted router to cut the cove inside the lip of the table

Photo 1

Photo 2

tops. Set the split fence ¾" from the outside of the cutter and raise the bit ⁷⁄₁₆" from the table for the first pass. (See photo 3.) With the good face of the tops up, begin cutting on an end-grain side and continue around each top. Then raise the bit to the height of the lip you cut in step 2, and cut around each top again.

4. Sand the table tops to 220 grit.

STARTING THE APRONS

1. Prepare stock for all the aprons. If you can thickness your ¾ cherry to 1⅛" instead of 1", by all means do so. You can get all of the aprons out of the following pieces: 4½" x 30", 3¼" x 32", and 2" x 32". This is the place to use that 11" x 32" hunk of ¾ that's been laying around all these years. Yeah, right. Once the wood is thicknessed, jointed, and ripped, go ahead and cut the aprons to length, accurately, using your drop stop. (See Drop Stops, Jigs, and Fixtures on page 12.)

2. Decide which edge of all apron pieces will be the bottom edge. On the bottom edge, mark 1¼" from each end on every apron. Put a ⁹⁄₁₆" bit in your drill press. Set the depth stop at 1⅞" from the table to drill countersinks for 2½" screws with ³⁄₁₆" washers. Drill countersinks, centered thicknesswise, at every mark.

3. Change to a ⁵⁄₁₆" bit in the drill press and bore through the aprons at every countersink. You did remember to put a scrap under your aprons, didn't you?

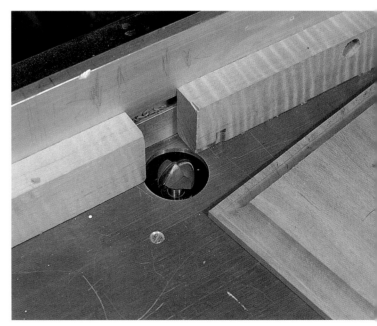

Photo 3

CUTTING THE LEGS

1. Leave the protective plastic wrapping on your balusters if they came wrapped: you bought the paint and you may as well keep it. The points on the corners of the balusters where the turning begins should end up ¼" below the bottoms of the aprons on each table. You will set the drop stop on your miter gauge to cut off part of the square end of the balusters, leaving the width of the aprons plus ¼" to the beginning of the turned portion. Here's how: Measure the distance from the square end of a baluster to the point on the corners where the turned part begins. (We'll call this the square length.) Subtract 4⅞" from that distance (width of large aprons plus ¼" plus ⅛" for the saw blade). Use the difference as the distance from the blade to the drop stop. To check your setting, put the end of a baluster against the drop stop and the miter gauge. Move the miter gauge until the baluster is near the (turned off) saw blade. Place an edge of a large apron (D) against the side of the blade away from the drop stop. There should be ¼" between the other edge of the apron and the beginning of the turning. (See photo 4, in which I'm cutting a short leg (K).) When you are satisfied with the set-up, cut the excess square portion from four large legs (I).

2. Subtract 3⅝" from the square length, and set the drop stop that far away from the blade. Check your set-up with a medium apron (E). Cut four medium legs (J).

3. Subtract 2⅜" from the square length, set the drop stop, and check your set-up with a small apron (F). Cut the remaining four small legs (K).

4. Using the drop stop set to the length of each set of legs as provided in the cutting list, cut the legs to length. The medium and small legs are ¼" less than you might expect so that those legs don't scuff the floor as they slide into their slots.

COMPLETING THE APRONS AND LEGS

1. With a 5/16" dado blade in the table saw protruding 5/16", set the rip fence to ¾" from the far side of the blade. Just to be clear, that's 7/16" from the near side. Lay out your large side aprons (D) and medium side aprons (E), with the good face up and with the top edge arranged so that you must cut near that edge. Cut a 5/16" x 5/16" groove the length of large and medium side aprons. (See photo 5, in which I have changed my rip fence to its low position.) Don't move that rip fence!

2. Use the miter gauge to guide two of the large legs (I) and two of the medium legs (J) while cutting grooves in one face of each leg. Do not cut grooves in the small legs (K) at all and cut only two each of the other sizes! (See photo 2.) If you delayed molding the edges of the tops in Making the Tops, page 52, now is the time to go back and finish them.

3. Refer to Biscuit Joinery on page 16 for a refresher course on this process. The small table has four identical legs and four identical aprons. On the top of each small leg (K), mark the two adjacent faces to receive slots. On one end of each small apron (F), place a mark indicating the good face. If you use your biscuit joiner upside down in a vise, as I do whenever possible, (see photo 11 on page 30) stack the small aprons with their good sides up. Set the

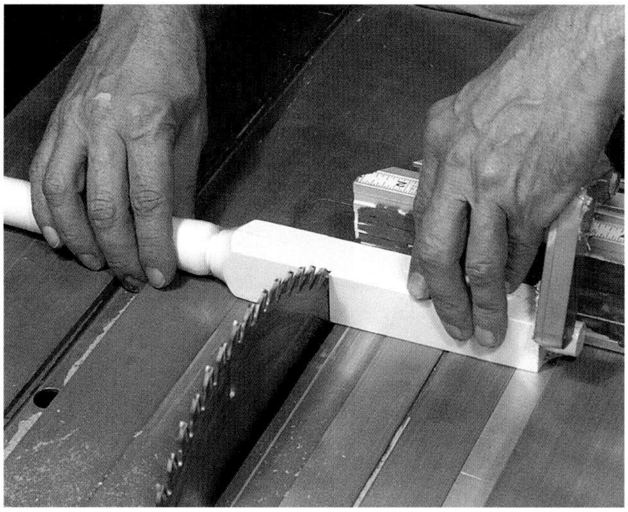

Photo 4

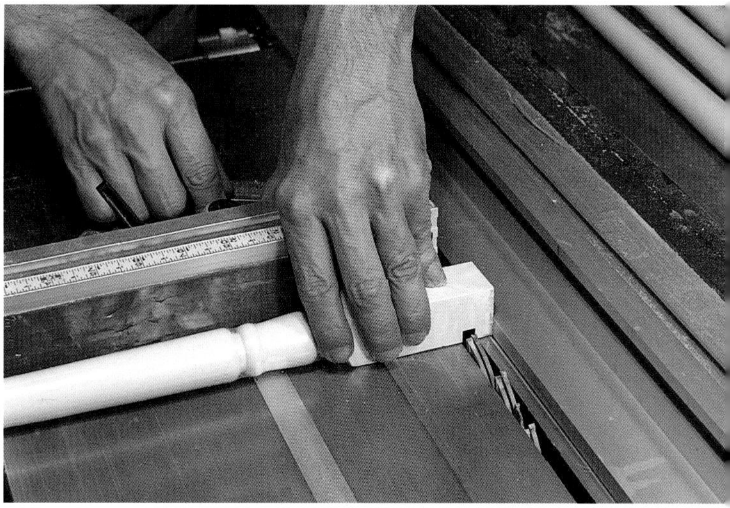

Photo 5

biscuit jointer to cut slots for #20 biscuits, and set the fence at ½". All the slots in all the aprons will be cut with the bottom edge of the apron at the mark for #20 slots on the bottom of the jointer. (If your biscuit jointer does not have this mark, draw one 1½" each way from the centerline of the base.) Since the #20 slot is larger than the 2" width of the small aprons, you must align the bottom edge at each end of each apron with the appropriate mark. The biscuit jointer will cut through the top of the apron. Cut a slot in both ends of the small aprons.

4. Hold the end of one small apron up to the biscuit joiner as you did to cut a slot, with its bottom edge aligned with the #20 mark. Make a mark on the jointer base even with the top edge of the apron. Turn the apron around and mark the other side of the jointer base at the top edge of the apron. These marks should be ½" on either side of the center line of the base. You will align the top ends of the small legs with these marks to cut matching slots in the legs.

5. Using your new marks, cut slots in the faces of the small legs you marked in step 3. Again, the cutter will

cut past the top end of the leg, so be careful. After you cut the first slot in each leg, turn it end-for-end and make sure that the first slot is facing down. The inside faces of the legs and the aprons are the index surfaces for all the joints in this project.

6. The medium side aprons (E) and the medium back apron (G) get slots in both ends. Cut these slots, with the inside faces of the aprons against the fence and with their bottom edges aligned with the #20 marks.

7. Mark the base of the biscuit jointer at the top edge of the medium aprons, as you did for the small aprons in step 4. These new marks will be ¼" outside the #20 marks on the base.

8. Cut biscuit slots in two adjacent faces of the two medium legs (J) without the 5⁄16" slots. Again, for the second slot, turn the leg end-for-end and make sure that the first slot faces down.

9. The front medium legs (those with the 5⁄16" slots) get one biscuit slot each, cut with the 5⁄16" slot down against the fence. They will align with opposite marks on the base.

10. Cut biscuit slots in both ends of the large side aprons (D) and the large back apron (F), following the procedure for the other aprons (step 6).

11. Since the top edges of the large aprons extend past the biscuit jointer base, they are difficult to mark with a pen. Instead tape a 6" ruler or a 6"-long anything centered across the base near the cutter edge. Use the ends of the ruler as your marks for the tops of the large legs (I). Cut biscuit slots in the back large legs as you did in step 8 for the back medium legs.

12. Finally, cut one biscuit slot in each of the front large legs, following the procedure in step 9.

FINISHING AND ASSEMBLY

1. Sand the aprons to 220 grit. Finish the aprons and tops completely now before any assembly. The burnished oil finish described on page 20 is a good choice for these parts. Rub and wax all of the cherry parts before proceeding. Go ahead. I'll wait.

2. Gather all the stuff you'll need: #20 biscuits, glue, legs and aprons matched for each table, clamps, pads, ruler, square, clear head, calm disposition.

3. Begin with the small legs and small aprons because they're the most fun. Pull the plastic down

past the joint area. You'll have to judge the biscuit position in these slots by the gap at the bottom end. If you're in doubt about how that should look, push a biscuit into a full slot in a medium apron, for instance, to get the idea. Glue the slots, push in biscuits, and assemble one side consisting of two legs and one apron. Make sure you have the top of the apron even with the tops of the legs and the inside face of all three pieces flush. Clamp it from the outside. With pads. Don't stop.

4. Glue, biscuit, and assemble another side, and clamp it. Don't stop.

5. Glue the remaining slots, push biscuits into the ends of the aprons, and push the two side assemblies onto the biscuits. Clamp those sides. Measure the diagonals to make sure that the assembly is square. Adjust the clamps until it's square. Now stop.

6. Lay out the medium aprons and the medium legs so that you'll surely assemble them correctly. Glue, biscuit, assemble, and clamp the two sides first. Then connect them with the back apron. Use your square as well as your ruler to make sure that the assembly is square and, especially, that the front legs are the same distance apart as the back legs. Adjust the clamp positions to correct any misapprehensions on the parts of the legs as to where they should be.

7. When you have free clamps, repeat step 6 with the large aprons and the large legs.

8. Use a dozuki or other fine-toothed hand saw to cut the excess biscuits flush with the top of the small base assembly.

9. Lay the three tops face down on a padded surface. Center each leg/apron assembly on its top. Push a ³⁄₁₆" washer into each countersunk hole. Use a power screwdriver, with the clutch set only high enough to set the screws, to drive 2½" screws into the tops. Pilot holes are generally not necessary for this operation. Make sure you hold the base assembly firmly in place as you drive the screws. Measure to check that the front and back legs of both the large and medium base assemblies are the same distance apart.

10. Stand the tables right-side up. Slide the medium table into the slots in the large table. Slide the small table into the slots in the medium table. Are you clever, or what?

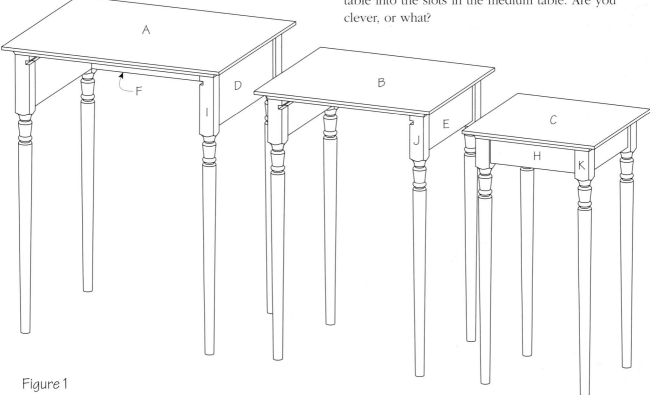

Figure 1

Glass-Top T Table

DESIGNED BY JOHN BICKEL

As much sculpture as it is furniture, this striking piece reduces the structure of a table to its minimum. The designer also makes this table with a wood top, which gives it a somewhat warmer feeling.

Materials

8/4 wenge

3/4" glass with polished edges

Cutting List

CODE	DESCRIPTION	QTY	MATERIAL	DIMENSIONS
A	Back	1	wenge	1 7/8" x 4 1/4" x 22"
B	Foot	1	wenge	1 7/8" x 4 1/4" x 18"
C	Top	1	glass	3/4" x 12 1/8" x 34"

(Do not order glass until you have completed the back (A), step 7.)

Important note on Materials and Sizes:
In order to make the instructions easier to read, I have used the dimensions of the table pictured. This table can be made from other 8/4 materials in other widths. While the dark color of the wenge presents a striking appearance, cherry and mahogany would also work, and may be easier to obtain in wide planks. If you can find and thickness a plank that is slightly wider or slightly narrower than the specified dimensions, feel free to use it. Note these important relationships: The slot in the back (A) is 1 3/4" shorter than the width of the plank. The width of the top (C) is 1/8" narrower than the length of the slot. If you can't find a wide, flat board, glue two narrower planks together to make a suitable width.

1. Flatten and thickness a wide 8/4 plank at least 42" long for the back (A) and the foot (B). Plane away only enough to clean the board. (Refer to Flattening, Thicknessing, and Jointing on page 8 for help.)

2. Joint one edge and rip or joint the other edge parallel to the first.

You must now choose between two alternative methods of cutting the slot in the back (A): routing (steps A3 to A6) or ripping/sawing/gluing (steps B3 to B6). Please read both options entirely before choosing one.

Option A: Routing the slot

A3. Square a line across the plank about 18 1/2" from one end. Work with the uncut 42" plank so that, in the unlikely event that you make a mistake in the first attempt, you have enough wood left to take another stab. The line you drew represents the bottom edge of the slot, which will be slightly wider than 3/4" and less than 13/16" wide. Draw a second line, exactly parallel with the first and a little more than 3/4" from it. That line will be about 19 1/4" from the end of the plank. Measure in 1" from each edge and draw a highly visible mark across those two lines. These two lines mark the ends of the routed slot.

A4. Use a 1/2" router bit long enough to extend through the plank, with a plunge router capable of a 1 7/8" depth-of-cut at minimum. (You could conceivably try to rout half-way from each face of the plank, but with a great likelihood of cutting two distinct slots.) Clamp a straight piece of plywood to the plank so that its edge is parallel to the nearer of the slot edges and the radius of your router base minus 1/4" away

from the slot. Clamp another piece of plywood with its straight edge the same distance outside the other marked edge of the slot.

A5. Cut less than ¼" of wood at a time, moving the router so that the cutter pulls the base against the appropriate fence. (For instance, if the fence is on your left, push the router away from you.) Lower the

bit by ¼" at a time, cutting the waste from the whole slot at each depth. When you get close to the opposite face, don't force the bit through—move the router and let the bit cut its way through.

A6. Draw lines parallel with the edges of the plank and ⅞" from the edge at each end of the slot on both faces of the board. Use a ½" or ¾" chisel, preferably a mortise chisel, to clean the ends of the slot. Don't try to remove all the waste at once, and work inward from both faces. Finally, pare away the last little bits so that the edges of the slot go straight to the corners all the way through the plank. Remember that you will be able to see into the slot even when the glass top is installed, so make it pretty in there.

Option B: Sawing the slot

B3. Cut a piece 23" long from your ¾ plank. Draw a slanted line across the face in what will be the lower half of the piece. This line facilitates reassembling the board. Rip a strip $^{15}/_{16}$" wide from each edge of the board. With one thin pass over the jointer, clean up the ripped edges for gluing. Set the two strips aside to be glued back on.

B4. Using your best crosscut blade on the table saw, cut square across 4" below the top of the board. Take this opportunity to sand the end grain on both sides of the cut you just made. Those surfaces are the top and bottom of the slot, so sand carefully, and don't round them over.

B5. Refer to figure 1. Reassemble the original board on a piece of paper or heavy plastic film, using the slanted line to align the strips with the main part of the board. Move the top piece until it is a little over ¾" away from the bottom piece. Find or make a gauge block which is an honest ¾" thick (no thinner).

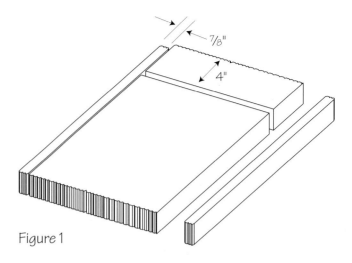

Figure 1

Use the gauge block now and during glue-up to make sure that the slot is slightly taller than ¾".

B6. Flop the two strips outward and apply glue to areas which will contact the two central pieces. Replace the strips, guided by the slanted line, and clamp the assembly together. Check the slot height with your gauge block. Make sure that the faces of all the pieces are flush. Use a straightedge to check that the faces of the central pieces are on the same plane. Do not try to remove squeezed-out glue from inside the slot; do so with a sharp chisel once the glue has dried.

7. Measure the length of the slot. Ideally, the glass top will be ⅛" narrower than the slot length. But think for a moment before you order the glass: In what way will the width of the back (A) change over the next year? If it's February and the lumber you're using has become acclimated to the warm and dry conditions of your shop in northern Minnesota, you can confidently order glass a scant ⅛" narrower than the length of the slot. If you expect your material to become drier, however, you should probably order glass ¼" narrower than the slot length. Make your calculations, adjust as you see fit, and order a piece of ¾" plate glass, (slot minus X)" wide and 34" long, finished with a polished edge.

8. Make your measurements for trimming the back (A) from the bottom of the slot. Cut the top end of the back 4" above the bottom of the slot. Cut the bottom end of the back 18" below the bottom of the slot. Sand the back completely.

9. Is the sawn end of the piece for the foot (B) square both to its faces and to its edges? If so, proceed. If not, make it so now. With the back (A) lying on your bench, position the foot so that it is equidistant from the edges of the back, and so that its squared end is flush with the bottom of the slot. Mark the length of the foot by tracing the bottom of the back with a sharp pencil onto the edge of the foot. Also trace one side of the edge of the foot onto the face of the back.

10. Cut the foot (B) to length. You have one chance to get this right, so squaring a pencil line across the face beforehand might be prudent. Sand the foot completely, except for the edge to be glued to the back.

11. A simple glue joint is strong enough to hold the back and the foot together, but you may wish to add biscuits (see Biscuit Joinery on page 16), as John Bickel does, to help align the two pieces. Clamp a board just outside the line you traced on the back (A) as a fence for the bottom of your biscuit joiner. Mark placement lines 2", 9", and 16" from the bottom of the back (A) and from the bottom of the foot (B). Cut three #20 slots into the back.

12. With the side of the foot (B) you traced in step 9 down on the bench, hold the bottom of your biscuit joiner flat on the bench while you cut the three slots into the edge of the foot.

13. Spread glue on the edge of the foot (B), insert three biscuits, put a little glue into the biscuit slots in the back (A), and press the two pieces together. Make certain to align the top of the foot with the bottom of the slot for the glass top. Apply pressure with bar clamps and check your alignment again. Check that the faces of the foot are square to the face of the back, too.

14. When the glue has set, scrape off any stray glue and resand those areas. Ease all the corners except those around the slot, which should be kept sharp. Finish the table with a burnished oil finish (see page 20) or another finish of your choice.

15. When the finish is dry and the glass arrives, slide the glass top (C) into the slot. Play with the proportions of the glass exposed on each side of the back until you are pleased with the result.

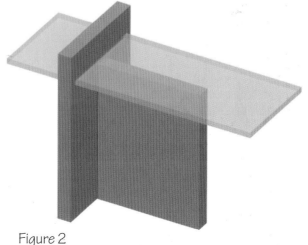

Figure 2

Triangle Table

DESIGNED BY RICHARD JUDD

This sprightly table stands on tiptoe to hold both your current novel and a small light by which to read it. If it's a very romantic novel, replace the lamp with a vase of flowers or even a candle.

Materials

¾ birdseye or curly maple

¾ wenge or cherry or walnut

Supplies

#6 x 2" drywall screws

Cutting List

CODE	DESCRIPTION	QTY	MATERIAL	DIMENSIONS
A	Legs	3	wenge	1¾" x 1¾" x 27"
B	Shelves	2	birdseye maple	¾" x 13½" x 17½"

Note: The look of this table depends on a sharp contrast between the colors of the shelves and the legs. Wenge contrasts well with the maple, and it is hard, splintery, and relatively expensive. Cherry and walnut provide a softer contrast, are easier to work, and are less costly.

MAKING THE LEGS

1. Since the shelves fit into the legs, you should make the legs first. Flatten, thickness to 1¾", and joint one edge of an ¾ plank at least 5" wide and 28" long. (See Flattening, Thicknessing, and Jointing on page 8 for help.)

2. Square one end of the plank with the table saw, and then cut the other end to 27" long.

3. At one end, mark points ⅛", 1⅞", 2", 2½", 2⅝", and 4⅜" from the jointed edge. At the other end of the same face, mark points ¾", 1¼", 1⅜", 3⅛", 3¼", and 3¾" from the jointed edge. With a long straightedge and a sharp pencil, connect the first marks you made at each end, then the second marks, and so on (see figure 1). You now have outlines for three legs tapered from 1¾" at the top to ½" at the bottom. If you have an adjustable tapering jig for your table saw (and a sharp rip blade), you might want to use it to saw these legs. This small job doesn't justify making special jigs.

4. Band saw between the lines that are ⅛" apart first. Then saw an equal distance outside the remaining two lines.

5. Remove the saw marks by passing the legs over a jointer set for a thin cut or by hand-planing.

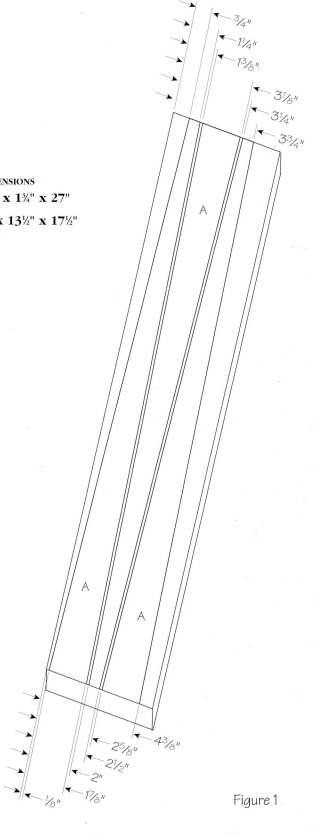

Figure 1

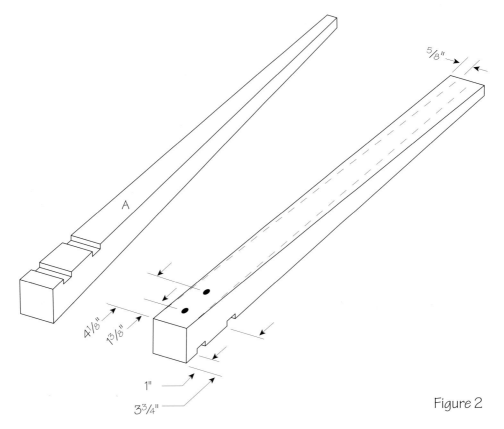

5/8"

A

4⅛"
1⅜"
1"
3¾"

Figure 2

6. Cut two dadoes on the inside face of each leg for the shelves. Each dado is ¾" wide and ¼" deep. They begin at 1" and 3¾" below the top of the leg, leaving 2" between the shelves (see figure 2). Notice that the dadoes are cut square into one of the tapered sides: the inside of each leg will be vertical. You kept two sides of the legs untapered to facilitate cutting the dadoes on the table saw with the help of a drop stop or the rip fence.

7. On the outside face of each leg, mark points 1⅜" and 4⅛" from the top, centered widthwise. Drill ⅜" countersinks, about ⅜" deep, and 9/64" clearance holes through to each dado.

8. With the dadoes facing down, mark ⅝" in from each edge at the bottom of the legs. Draw a straight line between those marks and the corners at the top of each leg (see figure 2). Saw the tapers and clean them up on the jointer or by hand.

9. Sand the tops and faces of all three legs. Using a low-angle block plane or 220-grit paper on a block, bevel the top corners of the legs (the sharp corner between the top and each face) no more than ⅛". Keep the corners of the bevels sharp. Ease the long corners and finish sanding. Richard sands everything to 600 grit. That's smooth!

MAKING THE SHELVES

1. Begin by making a triangular pattern with equal sides 17½" long. You can do this most accurately by using a large compass. Draw a straight line on a piece of matte board and mark two points 17½" apart on the line. Set the compass to that length and draw an arc from each point so that the arcs intersect. Finally, draw a line from each starting point to the intersection of the arcs. If you don't have a large compass or trammel points, you could use a length of dental floss tied to a pencil point and wrapped around a nail. Use a ruler and a matte knife to cut out the pattern.

2. You can see from the pattern that you will need stock at least 13½" wide, to be glued up from two 7" or three 5" boards. By offsetting the boards when you glue them, and by rotating the pattern, you can get by with two 7" boards 22" long (refer to figure 3). Choose your stock accordingly, and use the pattern to make sure you'll get two attractive shelves.

3. Flatten and thickness the planks to slightly over the width of the dadoes you cut in the legs. Check the thickness against the actual dadoes, not against a ruler, leaving a little extra for sanding. Then joint the edges for gluing.

4. With the boards arranged as you intend to glue them, use the pattern to make sure the offset is correct. Draw a pencil line across the joint to mark the positions of the boards. Glue them and clamp up. Check the pencil line and use a ruler on edge to check for flatness. (See Gluing Table Tops on page 10 for more tips.)

5. Belt sand the two faces to remove the remaining glue and to flatten the joint. Don't sand them thinner than the dadoes in the legs. Joint both edges again to straighten them and to remove clamping marks.

6. Choose the better face, mark it in the shelf areas, and trace your pattern on that side. With one side of the pattern flush with a jointed edge, trace two shelves at least ⅛" apart. Band saw midway between the shelves to separate them. If the throat of your band saw is not that wide, use a saber saw with a fine blade. Then stack the shelves with their jointed edges flush and the sawn edges even. Saw barely outside the lines on the top shelf. If the size of your band saw table allows, use a spring clamp to help hold the shelves together. Keep one of the cut-offs for plugs.

7. Keep those shelves clamped together! I know— you had to look. So realign them and spring-clamp them again. Put the shelves in a bench vise and belt-sand the edges to 220, keeping them square to the faces.

8. It's time to cut some corners. (Did you separate those two shelves? Again? Don't do that until I tell you to!) Because the legs taper, the lengths of the dadoes vary. Richard uses the length measured at the lower corner of the bottom dado. Refer to photo 1, which shows the correct fit: the corner of the shelf just inside the width of the leg. Measure all three legs at that point and use the average length. That's the

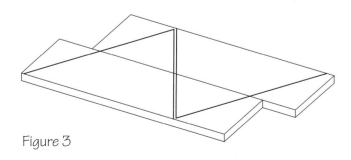

Figure 3

distance across the corners on the shelves. Use an adjustable square set to 60° and your best little ruler in combination to find that line and mark it with a sharp pencil.

9. With the shelves still stacked, saw to the lines. Check the lengths of the corners by holding the bottom of the lower dado against them. If the widths of your legs vary widely, you may wish to mark each corner for a particular leg. Use a low angle block plane or a sanding block to adjust the lengths of the corners. Planing the sides of the shelves shortens the corners and planing the corners lengthens them.

10. Now you can separate the shelves. Check their thicknesses against the dadoes, and use your finest sandpaper to reduce them to a good fit. And don't wimp out by sanding only at the corners: try to keep the shelves flat. The shelves should just slide into the dadoes without much force. Finally, ease the sharp corners between the shelf faces and edges.

ASSEMBLING THE TABLE

1. Use a ⅜" plug cutter in a drill press to make more than six plugs from your shelf cut-offs. The kind of plug cutter with four prongs works best.

2. If you haven't already done so, mark to indicate the top and bottom shelves and which legs go where. Make very sure that the shelves maintain their stacked relationship, with the grain lines running the same way. Working with each joint separately, center a corner in its dado and drill a short ⅜₂" hole into the edge of the shelf, through the screw hole in the leg. Don't touch the edge of the countersink with the drill

Photo 1

chuck. If your ³⁄₃₂" bit won't reach that far, use a nail to mark the edge of the shelf. Then remove the leg and extend the ³⁄₃₂" hole about 1" into the corner.

3. Are all five pieces sanded to a fare-thee-well? Good. Then begin assembling your table by driving a 2" drywall screw through one leg into the appropriate shelf. Attach the second shelf to the same leg and then add the remaining legs. Check that each corner is seated properly in its dado, and make sure that the screws are snug but not straining.

4. Dip each plug in yellow glue and press it into a countersink, with the grain of the plug parallel to the grain of the leg. Tap it home before going on to the next plug. A small square-headed tack hammer works well for this because it allows you to hit particular areas of the plug to keep it going straight in.

5. Let the glue dry. With plugs cut from figured wood, such as curly maple or birdseye maple, it is best not even to try paring away the excess stub, so great is the chance that it will break off beneath the surface of the leg. Sand the stubs off instead, using a block to avoid hollowing the surface, but be sure to get it flat and remove any puddled glue.

6. Finish the table as you wish. Refer to Burnished Oil Finish on page 20 for one good option.

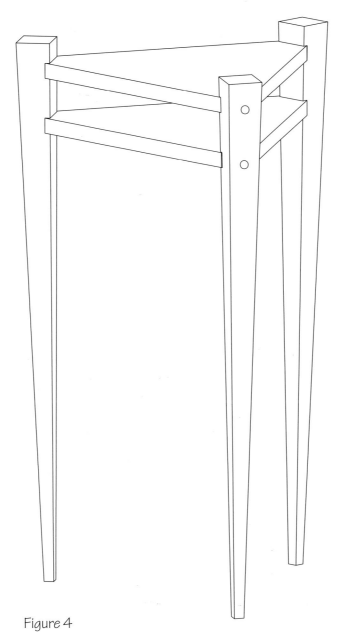

Figure 4

Magazine Table

DESIGNED BY THOMAS STENDER

I was looking for a way to keep partially-read magazines nearby without feeding one of those bins that, too quickly, begin to look like trash baskets. You could say that I tried to design my way out of a bad habit. This table is the result. It has modern lines that offer a good read while refusing to become overladen.

Materials

4/4 sassafras or oak

¼" birdseye maple veneered plywood

Supplies

#10 biscuits

3/16" washers

#6 x 1¼" drywall screws

#6 x 1⅝" drywall screws

Cutting List

CODE	DESCRIPTION	QTY	MATERIAL	DIMENSIONS
A	Top	1	sassafras	¾" x 16" x 22"
B	Panels	2	veneered plywood	¼" x 11½" x 17¾"
C	Legs	2	sassafras	⅞" x 3½" x 25¼"
D	Top arms	2	sassafras	⅞" x 2½" x 10¾"
E	Middle arms	2	sassafras	⅞" x 2½" x 13"
F	Lower arms	2	sassafras	⅞" x 2½" x 17"
G	Apron	1	sassafras	⅞" x 2½" x 17"
H	Back frames	2	sassafras	⅜" x 1" x 17"
I	Middle lip	1	sassafras	½" x 1¼" x 18¾"
J	Lower lip	1	sassafras	½" x 2" x 17"
K	Lower front	1	sassafras	¼" x 1⅜" x 17"

MAKING THE TOP AND PANELS

1. Flatten, thickness, and joint material for the top (A). (Refer to Flattening, Thicknessing, and Jointing on page 8 for help with this process.) Arrange the boards and joint them again for gluing. (See Gluing Table Tops on page 10 for tips.) Glue and clamp the boards for the top. Use double pipe clamps, or clamp on alternate sides of the top.

2. Joint one edge of the top, then rip it to just over 16", and joint the ripped edge. Cut the top to length. Sand the top to 220 grit or finer. You may finish the top using the burnished oil finish described on page 20, or wait until the rest of the table is ready.

3. If you are veneering your own ¼" panels (B), do so now. Cut the panels to size, and sand to 220.

MAKING THE SIDE FRAMES

You should draw a full-size version of figure 1. (See Fair Curves and Patterns on page 12 for help.) This will allow you to position the side pieces accurately.

1. Flatten, thickness, joint, and rip material for the legs (C), top, middle, and lower arms (D, E, and F), and the apron (G). You will cut and assemble the joints in these pieces before doing any shaping. Make sure that the arms are ripped accurately to 2½", because some of the following steps rely on that dimension.

2. Cut square across the top of each leg (C), and cut the top arms (D) to 10¾".

3. Cut a 25° angle at one end of each middle arm (E), and cut a 50° angle at one end of each lower arm (F). Yes, my miter gauge does go to 50°. If yours doesn't, you'll just have to go out and buy a table saw with larger adjustments. Or you might be able to put a wedge between your miter gauge and the lower arms to get to 50°. Check your work with a protractor and an adjustable bevel.

4. At what will be the front edge of the legs (C), measure down from the top and mark on one face 1¼", 6½", and 14½". These are centerlines for cutting biscuit slots.

5. Lay a leg on a flat surface with your marks from step 4 facing up. Butt a top arm against the leg with the top edge of the arm flush with the top end of the leg. Extend the mark on the leg onto the top arm.

6. Measure down 5" from the top of the leg, and position the top (acute) corner of a middle arm at that point, with its angled end against the leg. Extend the second mark from the leg onto the middle arm.

7. Measure down 12⅜" from the top of the leg, and position the top corner of a lower arm there. Extend the joint centerline as before.

8. Repeat steps 5 through 7 with the other pieces, stacking them atop the first set of leg and arms to make sure that both sides are the same. Before you move them, mark each set differently (R and L, for instance) so that you can reassemble the sides.

9. Cut the apron (G) to length (17"). On its back face mark 1¼" from one edge at each end of the apron. On the *inside* face of each leg (C) draw a line across the grain 1¼" from its top end.

10. With your biscuit jointer set to cut #10 slots, and its fence set at ⅜", cut the slots for all the arm-to-leg joints. With its front face against the fence, cut the slots in the ends of the apron. With their front edges against the fence, cut slots in the *inside* faces of the legs at the mark from step 9. There. The major joinery is done. Wasn't that easy?

11. Now bore the countersinks and clearance holes for the screws that will hold the top. On the lower edge of the apron, center marks at 1½" from each end and at the middle. On the lower edge of the top arms, mark 3" and 9¾" out from the joint end. Bore ⅜" countersinks to 5/8" from the top edge (1⅞" deep) at the marks near the fronts of the top arms only: these two holes get 1¼" screws. Bore countersinks to 1" from the top edge at the other five marks. Drill from the center of each countersink through the top edge of the top arms and the apron with a ³⁄₁₆" bit.

PICKING UP THE PIECES

1. Flatten, thickness, joint, and rip material for the back frames (H), the middle and lower lips (I and J), and the lower front (K).

2. The pieces surrounding the ¼" plywood panels all get ¼" x ⅜" rabbets on their lower inside corners to house the panels. Consult figure 1 to make sure you understand the orientation of each rabbet in pieces E, F, H, I, and J. These may be cut on the table saw or with a ball-bearing-guided ⅜" rabbet bit in a router table. In the latter case, use a split fence, especially with the thinner pieces. Use the edge of a panel to gauge the depth of the rabbet. It should be very

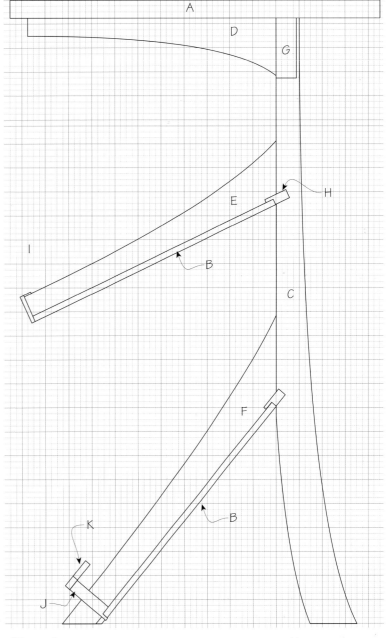

Figure 1   ¼ scale

slightly deeper than the thickness of the panels. Make sure to cut the rabbet on the insides of the arms: stack them beforehand so you know you're cutting opposite sides.

3. Assemble a middle arm (E) with a biscuit and its leg (C), matching the index lines. With the joint tight, slide the end of a panel into the rabbet with its back edge touching the leg, and mark its front edge on the arm. Stack the two middle arms and cut their front ends at this mark.

4. The back frames (H), lower lip (J), and lower front (K) will all be 17" long. Use the apron (G) to set the drop stop (refer to page 12) on your miter gauge and cut these pieces to length.

5. The middle lip (I) has ⅞" x ⅜" deep rabbets on its ends to cover the end grain of the middle arms. To make cutting these joints easier, first cut the middle lip to 18⅞" long. The space between the rabbets is 17", so use the apron again to mark this length, centered, on the rabbetted face of the middle lip. Cut to these lines with the table saw blade set just ⅜" high. Set the rip fence using the back of the panel rabbet as a gauge, and set the blade height to the middle of the kerf from the first cut. Then carefully cut off the waste piece by feeding the middle lip vertically past the blade, backed up with the square end of a piece of scrap.

6. One more loose end: saw and smooth a fair curve on one edge of the lower front (K). Leave ½" of width at the ends to cover the front edge of the lower lip (see figure 2).

ASSEMBLING THE SIDES

1. To clamp the joints on the middle arms and the lower arms, you need to cut a notch parallel with the joint on their outside edges. That's why you haven't cut the curves on the arms yet. But you don't want to cut into the finished arm area, so you must first draw those curves. Copy the curves from the full scale drawing to the arms and legs by making patterns for the three arms and the leg. Once the curves are marked, lay out the notches as shown in photo 1, and saw them out.

2. Lay a sheet of plastic over your drawing so that you can assemble each side on top of it. The top edge of the top arm, the front edge of the leg, and the bottom edges of the middle and lower arms should match lines on the drawing. Make sure that all that is so before beginning to glue. By the way, the slot for the apron is on the same side as the rabbets in the arms, right?

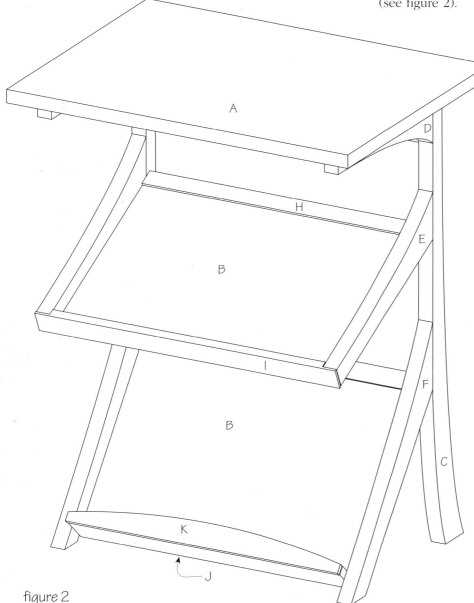

figure 2

3. Glue the slots in one leg, add biscuits, glue the slots in the arms for that leg, and clamp the joints closed. When you are convinced that the first side is flat and matches the drawing, glue up the second side.

4. Set the drop stop on your table saw to 25¼" from the blade. Cut the lower arm and leg to length as shown in photo 2 Support the arm as it goes past the blade and feed slowly.

5. Now, at last, it's time to saw the curves on the arms and legs. Just make sure that you don't cut into the leg when you're finishing the curves on the arms. Try to saw right up to the line to minimize smoothing.

6. Use a spokeshave and a low angle block plane to smooth as much of the edges as you can. Then finish up with sandpaper. Try to achieve fair curves, without humps or hollows.

7. Glue the lower front (K) to the front edge of the lower lip (J), with their bottoms flush.

8. Sand all the pieces of the table to 220 grit. (Except the top. That's finished already, right?)

FINAL ASSEMBLY AND FINISHING

1. Begin assembling the base by connecting the two sides with the apron (G). Work with the pieces upside down on your bench. When you have glued and clamped, check that the pieces are square by sliding a panel into the rabbets in the middle arms. Adjust the clamp if both corners of the panel don't meet the legs.

2. Spread a narrow line of glue on the wider part of the rabbets in the middle arms. Put a panel in place, face to the rabbets, and clamp the panel to the glued part of the rabbet. In other words, clamp from the bottom of the panel to the top curve of each arm. Use clamping pads to protect the arms. Make sure both corners of the panel touch the legs. Go directly to the next step.

3. Glue the wider part of the rabbet on a back frame (H) and clamp it in place. Again, the glue goes on the good side of the panel. Spring clamps work well here. Don't stop.

4. Spread glue in the rabbets of the middle lip (I) and slip it into place. Clamp it carefully, making sure that the joints close against the ends of the middle arms. Check the good side of the panel and try to remove any excess glue without spreading it around. Scraping with a sharp chisel works well for this, but wipe the chisel often. Then wipe the area hard with a paper towel. Finally, use a damp towel to wash away the glue you can't really see any more. It will surely show up when you apply the first coat of finish.

5. Install the lower panel, its back frame, and the lower lip in the same way. You need not put any glue on the ends of the lower lip. The rabbet joint will keep it in place.

6. Finish the base with a burnished oil finish (see page 20) or with another clear finish.

7. Place the top (A) and the base upside down on a padded surface. Push ³⁄₁₆" washers into the countersunk holes. Use a power screwdriver to install 1¼" screws through the two front holes in the top arms and 1⅝" screws through the other holes in the arms and the apron. You've earned the right to sit down and read a magazine.

Photo 1

Photo 2

Writing Table

DESIGNED BY GARY PETERSON

The design of this elegant writing table was influenced by the furniture of Charles Greene, an American architect who designed in the Arts and Crafts style. Gary tried to make efficient use of a limited quantity of exotic materials he had on hand. He has succeeded admirably.

Materials

4/4 greenheart

4/4 pernambuco

Alternate Materials: cherry with walnut, bubinga with wenge

Supplies

Table top fasteners with screws

1¼" screws

Cutting List

CODE	DESCRIPTION	QTY	MATERIAL	DIMENSIONS
A	Top Panel	1	greenheart	5/8" x 29" x 50⅜"
B	Cleats	2	pernambuco	13/16" x 3⅛" x 30½"
C	Legs	4	greenheart	1½" x 2½" x 28¼"
D	Knees	4	pernambuco	3/8" x 2½" x 8¼"
E	Long Aprons	2	greenheart	13/16" x 3½" x 42¾"
F	Short Aprons	2	greenheart	13/16" x 3½" x 22¾"
G	Stretchers	2	greenheart	13/16" x 2½" x 22¾"
H	Slats	6	pernambuco	5/8" x 1⅝" x 18"
I	Long Frames	2	greenheart	3/4" x 3¼" x 48⅞"
J	Short Frames	2	greenheart	3/4" x 3¼" x 20⅜"
K	Center Frame	1	greenheart	3/4" x 4" x 20⅜"

You will need the following loose tenons to be made from 3/8"-thick greenheart:

JOINT	QTY	DIMENSIONS	NOTES
top	2	3" x 4⅞"	
top	4	11/16" x 12⅜"	
long apron	4	2½" x 3⅜"	mitered on one end
short apron	4	2½" x 2⅜"	mitered on one end
stretchers	4	2" x 2⅜"	
slats	12	1" x 1⅞"	
short frames	4	2¼" x 2⅜"	
center frames	2	3" x 2⅜"	

NOTE ON CONSTRUCTION: Gary Peterson used mortise and loose tenon joints throughout his construction of this table, and I will follow his procedure in these instructions. For many of the joints, biscuit joinery may be used just as well (refer to Biscuit Joinery on page 16 for help). Traditional mortise and tenon joints would also work fine, but make sure to add the tenon lengths to the piece lengths provided.

MAKING THE TOP

1. Flatten, thickness, joint, and glue up enough ¼ greenheart for a top panel (A), ⅝" thick, 29" wide, and 50⅜" long. (See Flattening, Thicknessing, and Jointing on page 8 for helpful tips.) When the glue dries, trim the panel to those dimensions. Remove excess glue and sand the top panel smooth and flat to 220 grit.

2. Prepare two pieces of pernambuco for the cleats (B), $\frac{13}{16}$" thick and $2\frac{1}{2}$" wide. Make sure that one edge of each piece is smoothly concave lengthwise, about $\frac{1}{16}$" in 31". Cut the cleats to $30\frac{1}{2}$" long.

3. On each end of the top panel (A) and on each concave edge of the cleats (B), cut a mortise $\frac{3}{8}$" thick, 3" wide, and $2\frac{1}{2}$" deep, centered both thicknesswise and lengthwise. You may leave the ends of the mortise round.

4. On both sides of each of those mortises, and aligned with the mortises, cut a $\frac{3}{8}$" by $\frac{3}{8}$" slot outwards from the mortise $12\frac{1}{2}$". The slots stop $\frac{1}{2}$" from the edges of the top panel (A) and $1\frac{1}{4}$" from the ends of the cleats (B). See figure 1. This time, square the ends of the slots with a mortise chisel.

5. Prepare a length of greenheart tenon stock $\frac{3}{8}$" thick, about 4" wide, and about 72" long. The length could be made up from a couple of shorter pieces. Thickness this tenon stock to fit the mortises you have cut. As usual, it should present a sliding, unsloppy fit in the mortise.

6. Cut $12\frac{1}{4}$" from the tenon stock and from that piece rip four pieces $\frac{11}{16}$" wide.

7. You might want to round one edge of the remainder of the tenon stock now. Then cut $10\frac{1}{2}$" from the tenon stock, rip that piece to 3" wide, and round the other edge to fit the mortises you cut in step 3. Cut two tenons $4\frac{7}{8}$" long from this piece.

8. Assemble all the pieces you've prepared so far for a test-fit of the top. You should be able to close the joints between the top panel (A) and the cleats (B) using one double pipe clamp or two single pipe clamps on opposite sides of the top assembly. If the joints don't close, figure out why and fix it. Then remove the clamps and the two cleats.

9. The ends and the outside edges of the cleats (B) are rounded, as in figure 1. Saw the long curve on the outside edge first. At each end of one cleat, mark $\frac{1}{2}$" from the outside edge, and mark the center, lengthwise, of the outside edge. If you have a helper, bend a batten so that your assistant can draw a fair curve which hits all three points. (Refer to Fair Curves and Patterns on page 12 for help.) You cannot accomplish this by yourself unless you are tridextrous or a very skilled oral draftsman. Be sure to overbend the batten at the ends to arrive at a fair curve.

10. Saw to the curved line, and remove the saw marks with a plane. Use this cleat to trace the curved line on the second cleat, keeping the middle of the curve barely on the face of the second cleat. Again, hand-plane the curve smooth.

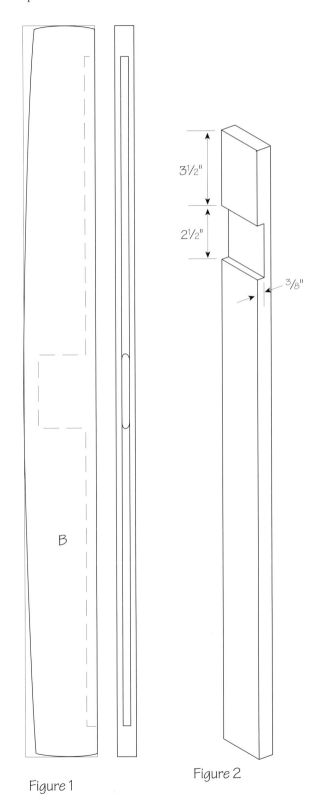

B

Figure 1

$3\frac{1}{2}$"

$2\frac{1}{2}$"

$\frac{3}{8}$"

Figure 2

11. The curves at the ends of the cleats are ⅛" deep, as shown in figure 1. You can sketch these freehand or find an appropriate circular object to trace. Band saw to the lines, or simply remove the waste with a rasp. Then file and sand the ends smooth, keeping the ends perpendicular to the top face.

12. Sand the cleats (B) to 220 grit on all surfaces except the inside edge. Touch up the top panel (A) if necessary.

13. Using a low angle block plane, chamfer the long edges of the top panel (A) ¹⁄₁₆" or ³⁄₃₂". Chamfer all the top and bottom edges of the cleats (B) by the same amount. Do a good clean job, and don't try to sand the chamfers. You have one shot to get this right, so practice first if you suspect you might need it.

14. Assemble the top again, gluing the center tenons in place. Do not glue the strips and slots. Clamp quickly across the center of the cleats, with even pressure on the top and bottom sides. Use a straight-edge to make sure that the faces of the cleats are parallel with the top of the panel.

MAKING THE PARTS FOR THE BASE

1. The legs (C) are made from two thicknesses of greenheart. Prepare enough material for eight pieces ¾" thick, more than 2½" wide, and longer than 28¼". Joint one edge of each piece, and cut all of them to length.

2. Sort the leg pieces for color and grain to get the best match between the two pieces in each leg. Mark the pairs on their ends with one through four slanted lines across the joint. Choose the piece from each pair which will end up closer to the middle of the table. You will cut a housing for the knee (D) into the glue face of each of these pieces.

3. Use a dado head on the table saw, with the miter gauge in combination with the rip fence or drop stop to cut a dado ⅜" deep and 2½" wide across the four inner leg pieces (see figure 2). The dado begins 3½" from the top of the leg and ends 6" from the top.

4. Prepare enough pernambuco for four knees (D). Thickness the stock to fit the dado's depth precisely, so that sanding the knees will produce a sliding fit. Joint one edge, then cut four pieces at least 8½" long. Rip and joint each piece to a sliding fit in a particular dado, marking the knees and inner leg pieces as you go.

5. Make a pattern for the knees (D) from the information in figure 3. Aligning the top edge and square end of the pattern with each knee blank, trace the curved line. Band saw to the line, then remove the saw marks with a spokeshave, file, and sandpaper. Sand the faces, curved edge, and square end of the knees.

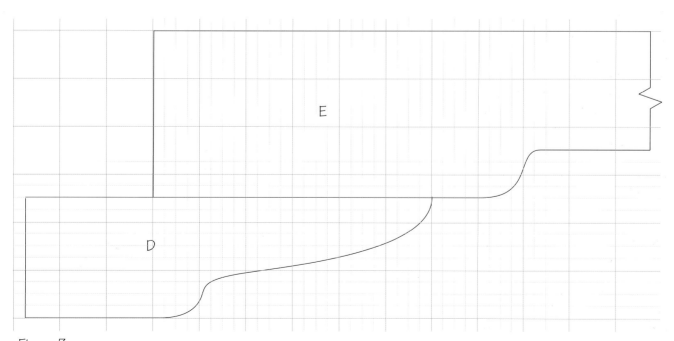

Figure 3   ½ scale

6. Carefully chamfer, by ¹⁄₁₆", the corners adjacent to the square end of each knee. Mark the bottom edge of each knee 2¾" from the square end. Chamfer the corners of the curved edge, ending just before the mark so that the chamfers won't enter the dado area. If you have a tiny spokeshave, use it to cut this curved chamfer. If not, you should use a sharp, narrow knife because the chamfers must not be sanded.

7. Use your slanted lines to match the leg pairs. Glue the inside faces, staying at least ½" from the dado area, and clamp the halves to cure. The ends of each pair must be exactly flush, and the jointed edges must be parallel and close to flush. When the glue is dry, joint the jointed edge again and rip and joint each leg to 2½" wide. Use a sharp chisel to remove any glue from the slot for the knee.

8. Cut mortises in the legs (C) for the aprons (E and F) and stretchers (G). The mortises at the tops of the legs are 2½" high and begin ½" from the tops of the legs. They are ⅜" wide, beginning ⁹⁄₁₆" from the outside faces of the legs. The mortises overlap inside the legs, 2" long into the narrow face and 1" long into the wide face. The mortises for the stretchers (G) are 2" high, ⅜" wide, and 1¼" deep, cut from 4½" to 6½" from the bottoms of the legs on the inside wide faces. Refer to figure 4.

9. Sand all faces of the legs (C), taking care to keep the joint areas flat. Finally, chamfer all four long corners of each leg ⅛".

10. Prepare greenheart stock for the long aprons (E) and the short aprons (F). Thickness all four pieces to ¹³⁄₁₆", and rip and joint all four pieces to 3½" wide. Cut the long aprons to 42¾". Cut the short aprons to 22¾".

11. Choose and mark the outside face of each apron. Cut ⅜" thick by 2½" wide by 1½" deep mortises in both ends of each apron. The mortises should be centered widthwise and should begin ⅛" from the outside face of the aprons. Refer to figure 5.

12. Make a pattern for the curved, bottom edge of the long aprons (E) using the information in figure 3. Trace this pattern on both ends of both long aprons and connect the curved areas with a straight line 2½" from the top edge of the aprons.

13. Band saw to the line, and remove the saw marks with spokeshave, file, plane, and sandpaper. Sand both faces and the curved bottom edge of the long

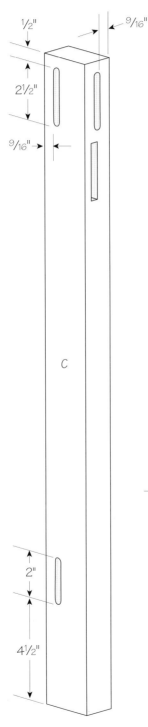

Figure 4

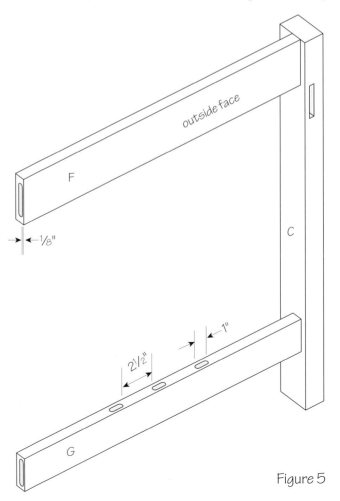

Figure 5

aprons, leaving the first 6" at each end of the bottom edge unsanded. Chamfer the corners of the bottom edges of the long aprons ¹⁄₁₆", using a narrow knife where necessary.

14. Prepare greenheart stock for the stretchers (G). Thickness both pieces to ¹³⁄₁₆", and rip and joint both pieces to 2½" wide. Cut the stretchers to 22¾".

15. Choose and mark the outside face of each stretcher. Cut ⅜" thick by 2" wide by 1½" deep mortises in both ends of each stretcher. The mortises should be centered widthwise and should begin ⅛" from the outside face of the stretchers. Refer to figure 5.

16. Stack the short aprons (F) and the stretchers (G), ends even, so that the bottom edges of the aprons and the top edges of the stretchers are flush and facing you. Measure 11⅜" from either end to mark the center, lengthwise. Measure ½", 3", and 4" out from the center on both sides to mark the lengths of the three slat mortises. Square those lines across the edges to mark all 12 mortises. Cut ⅜" mortises, 1" deep, and centered thickness-wise, in all of the marked, 1" long spaces.

17. Sand the faces and edges of the short aprons (F) and stretchers (G) to 220, being careful to keep the mortised edges flat and square. Chamfer the long corners ¹⁄₁₆".

18. Flatten, thickness, joint, and rip pernambuco stock for the six slats (H), then cut them to length. Cut ⅜" mortises, 1" deep and 1" long, centered both ways, into the ends of the slats.

19. Sand the faces and edges of the slats (H). Chamfer the long corners ¹⁄₁₆".

20. Find your tenon stock again. Here's a list of the remaining tenons you'll need:

Long apron	4	2½" x 3⅜"	mitered on one end
Short apron	4	2½" x 2⅜"	mitered on one end
Stretchers	4	2" x 2⅜"	
Slats	12	1" x 1⅞"	

Figure out how to get them out of the stock you have, cut them, and round the edges. Miter one end of each of the apron tenons so they will meet inside the leg.

ASSEMBLING THE BASE

I am about to tell you how to assemble all the pieces you've accumulated in the previous section. I will do this once. However, you will assemble the base twice (at least). Make sure that you assemble each section of the base dry, without glue, to make sure that all the joints fit accurately. Once you know that it will go together, proceed with the following steps again, adding glue in the appropriate places and waiting for it to set. During this process, it will be well to think only pleasant thoughts.

1. Lay out the parts for one end of the base: two legs (C), one short apron (F), one stretcher (G), three slats (H), and the appropriate tenons. Place the pieces as in an exploded view, so that there is no question later about which end goes up, down, left, or right. Is everything arranged properly? Are you sure?

2. Begin the assembly by applying glue inside the slat mortises in the stretcher (G) and its matching short apron (F), pushing in tenons as you go. Then apply glue inside the mortise on the bottom end of each of the three slats (H), and push each onto its tenon as soon as it's glued.

3. Glue inside the top mortises of the three slats, and start the apron tenons into their mortises. Clamp this assembly together with two clamps even with the outer two slats, but not outside the slats. Use a straightedge to make sure that the apron and the stretcher are in the same plane. Adjust the clamps until they are. Use a framing square to make sure that the ends of the apron and stretcher are even. Adjust the clamps until they are.

4. Glue inside the leg mortises for the short apron and the stretcher, pushing in the appropriate tenons as you go. Make sure the long side of the apron tenons are toward the outside of the leg.

5. Glue the mortises on one end of the apron and the stretcher. Push the leg tenons into place on that side. Repeat for the other side and clamp in line with the apron and the stretcher. Check to make sure that the mortised faces of the legs (where they will join the long aprons (E)) are even with each other. Also, sight across the assembly to make sure it's not twisted.

6. Repeat steps 1 through 5 to assemble the other end of the base.

7. Glue the leg mortises for the long aprons, and install the tenons with their long faces toward the outsides of the legs. Fetch your long pipe clamps and make sure you have pads for them. Clear enough space on your large work table or on the floor. This would also be a good time to call for a helper.

8. Match the knees (D) with their legs. Run a line of glue across the faces of one knee about ½" from the square end. Push the square end of the knee into the inboard end of its slot in the leg. Keep pushing until ¼" of the square end protrudes from the outside of the leg. Most of the glue should have been drawn into the slot with the knee, but make sure to clean up any visible glue right now, being careful not to spread it around. Use a wet paper towel to clean all glue from the surface of the wood. Install the other knees right away.

9. Don't stop to admire your work! Glue inside the mortises in the long aprons, and run a narrow line of glue on the top edges of the knees. With the base pieces all upside down, push the aprons onto their tenons. Try to avoid contact with the knees as long as possible to avoid spreading glue around. Clamp along the length of the aprons to close the joints. Quickly check that the legs stand square to the top edge of the aprons and that the top edges of the knees contact the bottom edges of the aprons. Clamp the knees to the aprons, and again make sure that the legs are square to the aprons. Measure the diagonals between opposite legs to make sure that the base is square horizontally. Adjust the clamps and push and pull until the two diagonals match. There. Wasn't that exciting? Cross your fingers and sit down.

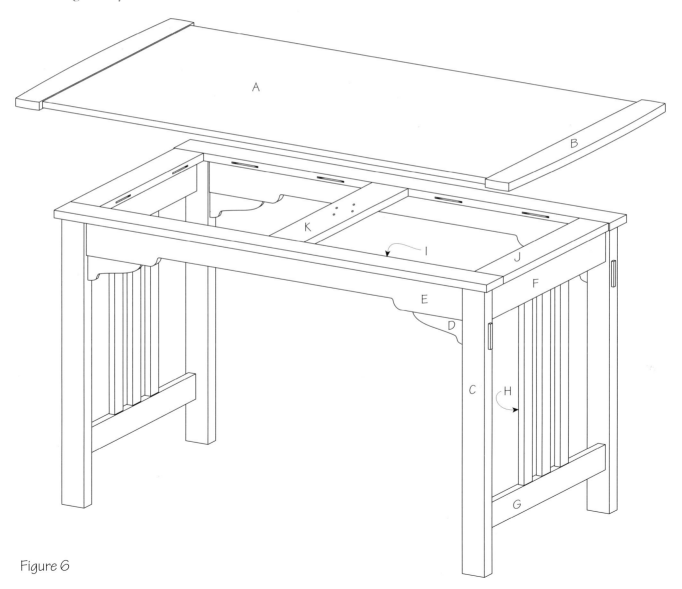

Figure 6

FRAMING, FINISHING, ASSEMBLING

1. A greenheart frame lies between the top and the base, providing a visual transition and a means of attaching the two main parts of the writing table to each other (refer to figure 6). The frame extends past the long and short aprons (E and F) by 1" on all four sides. You may wish to check the measurements that follow against your base, just to make sure. Begin by preparing greenheart stock for the frame pieces, finishing with the following dimensions. All of the pieces are ¾" thick. The long frames (I) and the short frames (J) are 3¼" wide, while the center frame (K) is 4" wide. Cut the long frames to 48⅞" long. Cut the short and center frames to 20⅜" long.

2. Cut mortises for the joints between the short frames and the long frames. These are ⅜" mortises, centered thicknesswise, 2¼" wide and 1¼" deep. Cut a mortise ½" from each end of the inside edge of each long frame. Cut a mortise centered in both ends of both short frames.

3. Find the center of the inside edge of each long frame, and then mark 1½" to both sides of the center. Cut 3" wide mortises 1¼" deep between the marks. Then cut similar mortises centered in the ends of the center frame.

4. Cut six tenons and round their edges: four 2¼" wide and 2⅜" long, two 3" wide and 2⅜" long.

5. Gary Peterson uses table top fasteners engaging slots on the inside edges of the long and short frame pieces. Cut slots for the fasteners now, two in each short frame and four in each long frame, distributed evenly (see figure 6). You could use 1¼" screws with fender washers through oversize holes near the inside edges of the frame pieces instead of the table top fasteners.

6. Assemble the frame dry and lay it atop the base assembly. It should overhang the aprons by 1" on each side. Keeping the pieces in order, disassemble the frame, then glue and assemble as before. You will need three clamps aligned with the short and center frame pieces. Make sure the frame assembly is flat.

7. Sand the frame assembly to allow it to lie flat against the top of the base and the underside of the top. Sand the exposed portions to 220. Plane a chamfer slightly less than ¼" wide on the lower outside corners all around the frame assembly.

8. Run a thin line of glue along the top edges of the long and short aprons on the base. Carefully place the frame assembly on top of the base, trying to position it correctly on the first try. A prudent worker would probably find a sensitive and caring helper for this step. Make sure the frame overhangs the aprons by 1", and then clamp it in place until the glue cures.

9. While the glue cures, drill four ³⁄₃₂" holes at the corners of a 3" by 8" rectangle centered on the center frame (refer to figure 6). These will accommodate 1¼" screws anchoring the middle of the top to the frame.

10. Finish the base and the top using the burnished oil finish method described on page 20 or your method of choice.

11. Place the top upside down on a padded surface. Center the base assembly upside down on the top, and mark the 16 screw positions on the top. Move the base enough to allow drilling ³⁄₃₂" pilot holes no more than ½" deep into the underside of the top. Put the base back in position and fasten the frame to the top.

Outdoor Stacking Tables

DESIGNED BY THOMAS STENDER

These handsome tables go together easily without mechanical fastenings, and they stack four high for compact storage. The design is forthright and efficient of materials. That's another way of saying that they're simple and cheap.

Materials

¾ cedar (one ¾ x 12" x 10' yields two tables)

Supplies

#20 biscuits

Structural epoxy

Cutting List

CODE	DESCRIPTION	QTY	MATERIAL	DIMENSIONS
A	Legs	4	cedar	1" x 2" x 20"
B	Aprons	4	cedar	1" x 2" x 14"
C	First Top Slats	2	cedar	⅜" x 3" x 25¼"
D	Second Top Slats	2	cedar	⅜" x 3" x 18¾"
E	Third Top Slats	2	cedar	⅜" x 3" x 12¼"
F	Fourth Top Slats	2	cedar	⅜" x 3" x 6"

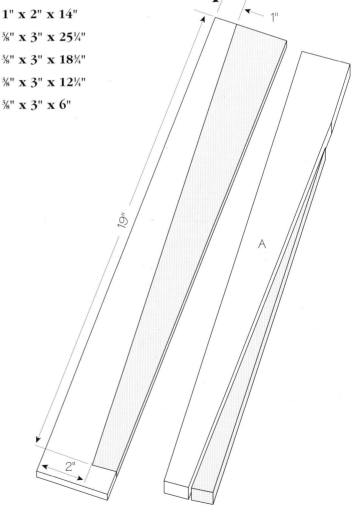

Figure 1

IMPORTANT NOTE:

Since these tables can stack four high, it's reasonable to allow you to make four tables for your own use only. But please do review the rights reserved statement on page 4 and my discussion of it on page 23.

That being said, if you plan to make more than one table, by all means make them all at once. This project lends itself to multiple production. I will describe the procedure for making one table, just to keep things simple.

MAKING THE LEGS AND APRONS

1. Plan how to get all the pieces for the table most efficiently from the stock you have. Notice that the top slats are resawn. You will probably have to work around some knots.

2. Flatten, thickness, joint, and rip 2" strips for the legs (A) and the aprons (B). If you can't get 1" of thickness from the cedar, make the pieces as fat as you can. They must all be the same thickness and they should be at least ⅞" thick. (See Flattening, Thicknessing, and Jointing on page 8 for review.)

3. Cut four legs (A) to length, 20", using the drop stop on your table saw. Cut four 14" aprons (B) while you're there.

4. You may wish to make a simple taper jig for the legs from ½" or ¾" plywood. Refer to figure 1. Begin with a piece of plywood at least 3" wide and 21" long. Make a pencil mark 1" from one end and 1" from one edge. Make another mark 19" from the same end and 2" from the same edge. Use a framing square to connect the two marks, extending the line off the far end of the plywood, and to square from that line to the

Photo 1

Photo 2

edge from the 1" x 1" mark. Band saw precisely to the lines, removing the shaded area in figure 1.

5. The legs taper from full width at 2⅛" from the top to 1" wide at the bottom. With the taper jig against the rip fence on the table saw, and the hook end nearest you, put one of the leg pieces in the jig, tight against the hook. Adjust the fence until a point 2⅛" from the far end of the leg just touches the near end of the blade. Remove the leg piece, and push the jig along until you can measure out from the hook. That distance should be pretty close to 1", but the place where the blade enters the wood is more important. Refer to photos 1 and 2, where I use a push stick to feed the jig and the leg past the blade, and my other hand to hold the leg against the jig. Remember that the top side of the leg as it lays in the jig will be the good side of the leg. Taper all four legs.

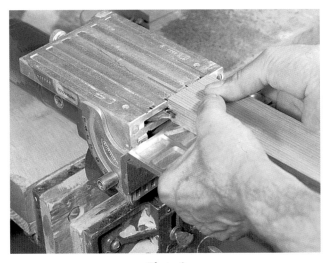

Photo 3

Photo 4

6. Using #20 biscuits in 2"-wide material means that part of the biscuit will protrude from the top of the joint, but more biscuit is in the joint than if you use a smaller size. It will be easiest to control the cut if you mount your biscuit jointer in a bench vice. Cut the aprons (B) first, good face down against the fence. Set the fence so that the slot is near the middle, thicknesswise, of the aprons and legs, but not centered. The off-center slot will serve to indicate which is the good side of each piece and prevent mistakes in the heat of gluing.

7. Stack all your aprons good face down, within reach. Put all blemished edges on one side of the stack and mark the edges of that side. Those will be the top edges. Align the bottom edge of each apron with the appropriate #20 line on the base of the jointer. If your biscuit jointer does not have those lines, which are 3" apart, draw them now, each 1½" from the centerline. Refer to photo 3, where the top edge of the apron is visible. Cut slots in the ends of all the aprons, switching guidelines as you turn each piece, and keeping the good face down.

8. Before you move the stack of aprons, use one of them to mark the base of the biscuit jointer where the top edge of the apron landed when you cut the slots. These lines will be ½" from the centerline on the base, and they will mark the top ends of the legs. On each leg (A) you will cut a slot in the straight, top end of the tapered edge and another slot in the back face near the untapered edge. Stack the legs face down with the tapered edge away from you. Cut the slots in the 2⅛" top edge with the top end aligned with the right-hand mark.

9. Turn the stack of legs end-for-end and twist it so that the untapered edge is down and the good side faces you. Cut the second slot in the back face of each leg, top aligned with the left-hand mark, as shown in photo 4.

10. Sand the tapered edge of each leg, but not the joint area, to 220 grit.

11. Structural epoxy works best for the joints in this table, especially if it will be left outdoors (see Structural Epoxy on page 19), but you can use yellow woodworking glue instead. If you do, this would be a great time to try one of the relatively new exterior formulations of woodworking adhesives.

12. Apply glue to the slot on the edge of a leg and to the left slot on an apron. Push the joint together after inserting a #20 biscuit and clamp across the joint (see photo 5). Use a straightedge to make sure the two pieces are flush and untwisted. Assemble the rest of the legs to one apron in the same way.

13. When the glue has cured, sand all the pieces to 220 grit, except the joint area on the legs. Then glue up and assemble the table, clamping as you go. Use a ruler to check the diagonal measurements to assure that the table base assembly is square. If it isn't, adjust the clamps.

14. When the glue has cured, trim the excess biscuits flush with the tops of the legs and aprons, as shown in photo 6. Sand the joints you just glued and ease the corners on all the corners except those which will contact the top slats.

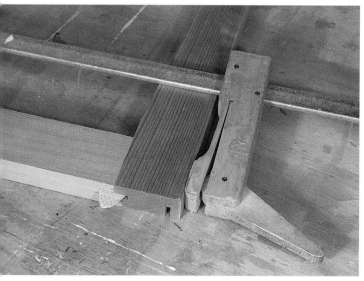

Photo 5

Photo 6

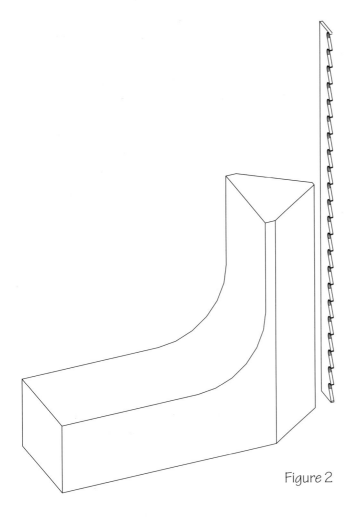

Figure 2

MAKING THE TOP SLATS AND COMPLETING THE TABLE

1. One piece of ¾ cedar 3" x 55" yields enough material for the top slats if you don't cut them until you must. Flatten, thickness as fat as possible, and joint ¾ cedar for the top slats. Rip the cedar to 3" wide.

2. Resaw the cedar with a band saw. A ½", 3-tooth hook blade works best. In fact, I keep this blade on my machine all the time. If you do not have one, make yourself a resaw guide, as shown in figure 2. Clamp the guide to your band saw table so that the pointed edge of the guide is even with the front of the blade teeth. Since the band saw blade is flexible, it can twist slightly while cutting. A difference in the way the teeth are sharpened from one side of the blade to the other, or changing grain patterns in the wood, can cause the blade to tend to cut to the right or the left. The very short fence of the resaw guide allows you to change your angle of feed to keep the blade cutting in the center of your stock, even if the blade wants to lead one way or the other.

3. Thickness the resawn stock to ⅜" or as thick as you can.

4. Make a simple jig from scraps to establish the border of an 18" square, as shown in photo 7, where I have clamped some pieces and nailed others to my work table. Begin cutting the top slats with the fourth top slats (F), by mitering them to a point. Put them in opposite corners of your jig.

Photo 7

Photo 8

Figure 3

5. Cut the first top slats (C) next. Miter both ends of both slats to the length of the diagonal dimension of your jig, then trim them until they leave a ³⁄₁₆" gap when placed against the sides of the jig. (The dimensions for top slats in the Cutting List have been checked but are not guaranteed.)

6. Hold a mitered end of your slat material against the side of the jig, with the new slat ³⁄₁₆" from a first

top slat (C). Mark at the other side of the jig and cut the second mitered end for a second top slat (D). Try and trim as before, then cut your second second top slat. (Could these names be more confusing? Sorry.)

7. Hold a mitered end of your slat material against the side of the jig between a second top slat and a fourth top slat. If the gaps look like the gap between the first and second slats, mark and cut as in step 6. If not, even things out, mark anything that needs changing, and cut to fit. Do the same with the other side of the table.

8. Cut an 18" square from scrap ½" or ¾" plywood. Turn the good sides of all top slats down and arrange them again on the plywood square. Place the leg/apron assembly upside down and centered on top of the slats. Make sure that the slats are still arranged properly. Hold each apron down firmly and trace each onto the slats. Remove the base assembly. Mix up a small batch of structural epoxy and spread it in a narrow path down the center of the apron outlines, as shown in photo 8.

9. Carefully put the base assembly back in place. Clamp the base assembly lightly to the top slats (and the plywood) as shown in photo 9. You can clean up epoxy that squeezes out on the slats, but be careful not to spread it farther, and don't push it into the gaps between the slats. When the glue cures, your table is complete. I'm using mine without finish, but you can use an exterior oil finish if you wish. Or wait until you need to hide the potato chip stains. Enjoy!

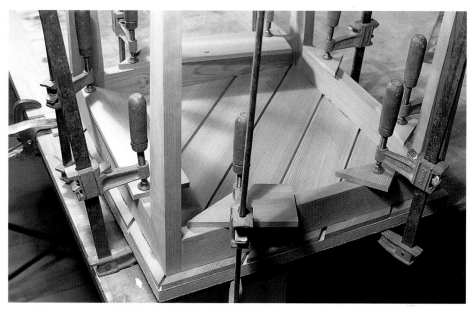

Photo 9

New Works Table

DESIGNED BY MARK C. TAYLOR

Exercise your design skills on the top of this table. Rearrange the stripes and dots until they're just right for you. Then display your expression proudly.

Materials

¾ walnut

¾ maple

¾ ash

¾ poplar or maple

⁸⁄₄ poplar or maple

Supplies

Table top fasteners and screws

Corner brackets and screws

#20 biscuits

Cutting List

CODE	DESCRIPTION	QTY	MATERIAL	DIMENSIONS
A	Top	1	walnut	¾" x 18½" x 18½"
B	Stripes	3	maple	⅜" x ¾" x 24"
C	Dots	5	ash	½" diameter plugs
D	Legs	4	poplar or maple	1½" x 1½" x 28¼"
E	Aprons	4	poplar or maple	¾" x 2½" x 13½"

MAKING THE TOP

The top of this table distinguishes it, so you should take special care to lay out the stripes and dots in a pleasing pattern. Mark Taylor says that the solution shown here is not definitive—he urges experimentation. I have provided the measured layout to give you a head start. Some cautions are in order. Be sparing with the number of stripes and dots. This top requires cross-grain joinery, but avoid running stripes at greater than 45° to the grain lines of the top. Walnut is a good choice for the top because it expands and contracts less than other domestic woods. Mahogany would serve well, too.

1. Flatten, thickness, joint, and edge glue material for the top (A). (Refer to Flattening, Thicknessing, and Jointing on page 8 and to Gluing Table Tops on page 10 for help.) Cut the top square but oversize, say 19" on a side, to allow for slippage while gluing the stripes.

2. Prepare three maple stripes (B) and five ash or maple dots (C). Cut the dots with a ½" plug cutter mounted in a drill press. The four-pronged kind of plug cutter works best.

3. Place the stripes and dots in position on the top. Where the stripes cross, simply let one lay atop the other. Notice how varying the placement of the various elements changes the composition. Mark the position of every piece when you are satisfied with your layout. Refer to figure 1 for Mark Taylor's arrangement.

4. Begin with the stripes. You will cut the top and glue in one stripe before moving on to the next stripe. Lay the top on your table saw, using a straight-edge to align the mark for the first stripe with the

blade. Slide the miter gauge up to the table top and adjust the fence to the angle of the top. Holding the top firmly against the miter gauge, cut through the center of the marks for the first stripe. Joint the cut edges, working with the grain, of course.

5. Place a stripe (B) between the realigned pieces of the top. At three evenly-spaced points, mark from one side of the top square across the stripe onto the other side of the top. You will cut the outer slots through the stripe into one side of the top, and the middle slot through the

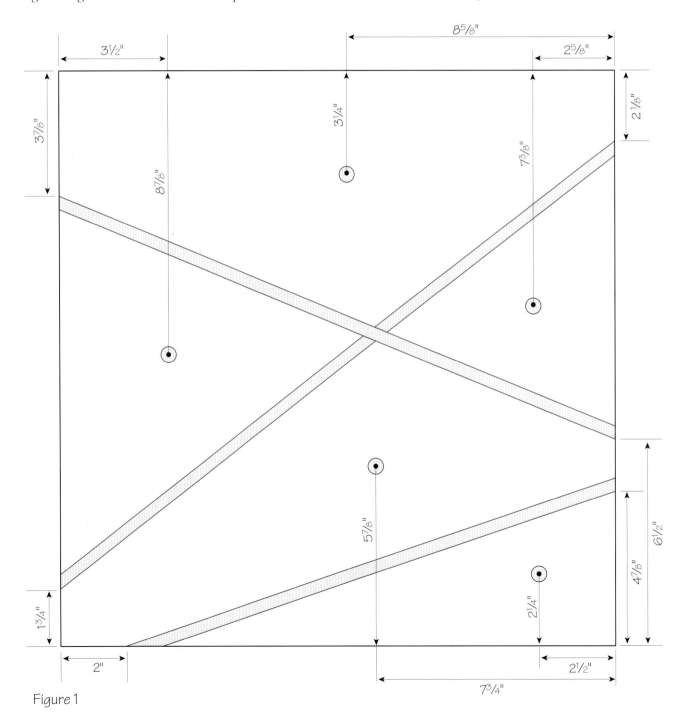

Figure 1

stripe into the other side of the top. Use arrows to mark the opposing directions of the slots which go through the stripe into the two parts of the top. Photo 1 shows the arrangement of the alternating slots.

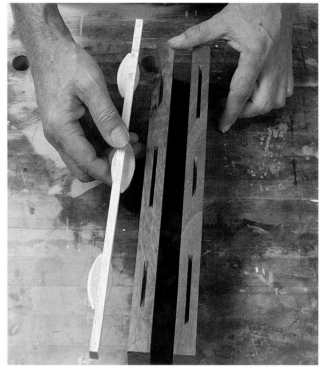

Photo 1

Photo 2

6. Cut the slots with the joiner set for #20 biscuits. Clamp one part of the top and the stripe, with marks aligned, to a flat surface. With most joiners you can use the base of the machine against the surface to cut the slots nearly centered in the edge of the wood. Cut slots at the marks with arrows on the top. Then remove the strip and cut slots at the marks with no arrows. Clamp the other top piece, with the strip aligned, to the bench. Again, cut slots through the stripe at the marks with arrows on the top, and without the stripe at marks with no arrows. Photo 2 shows the sample pieces being test-fitted.

7. Glue up the edges of the top and the slots. Push biscuits into the top pieces at the arrows, and align the stripe with the marks on one top piece. Push the other top piece into place. Use double pipe clamps if you have them (or opposing bar or pipe clamps) to compress the joints. You may have to use a bar clamp at a right angle to the main clamps to keep the pieces from sliding out of position. Make sure that the table top is flat, and adjust the clamps if necessary.

8. When the glue in the first stripe joints has set, sand to clean up stray glue, and repeat steps 4 through 7 to glue in the second stripe. Repeat again for the third stripe.

9. Bore ½" holes ⅜" deep at the marks you made for the dots. Test your drill bit on a scrap to make sure that it cuts a clean hole without tearing the surface of the wood.

10. Dip each dot (C) in a puddle of glue and start it into a hole, aligning its grain with that of the top. Use a hammer to knock each one down snug. When the glue has cured, carefully pare off the protruding plugs. Do not try to whack off the excess with one mighty blow. If you guess wrong as to the plug's grain direction, you will leave a hole in the surface.

11. Sand the faces of the top to get rid of excess glue and to flatten them. Then cut the top to its final dimensions: 18½" square.

12. With a low-angle block plane or a 45° bevel bit in your router, chamfer the top and bottom corners of the table top ³⁄₁₆" deep, leaving a ⅜" square edge.

13. Sand the top to 220 grit, keeping the chamfers sharp. Finish the top with a burnished oil finish (see page 20) or another clear finish.

MAKING THE LEGS

1. Prepare 1½" square poplar or maple stock for the legs (D). Cut the ends to produce 28¼" pieces.

2. The two inside faces of the legs are tapered to ¾" square at the bottom. The outside faces remain straight. The taper begins 2¾" from the top of the leg. You may wish to make a taper jig to cut the legs with a ripping blade on the table saw, as illustrated on page 80. You could also draw the lines on each leg, cut them slightly outside the line with a band saw, and clean the sawn faces on the jointer. There are only four legs, so both methods would take about the same time.

3. Chamfer the inside corner at the top of each leg about ¼" wide to make the pilot hole for the bracket screw easier to start. (That is, if you're using brackets. See Joinery Options below.)

4. Sand the legs to 220, easing the corners slightly, and taking care to keep the inside faces at the tops of the legs flat and square.

JOINERY OPTIONS

Mark Taylor uses corner brackets to hold the legs and aprons together and table top fasteners to hold the aprons to the top. This is a very direct method of joinery and facilitates shipping his tables. You may choose to join the legs to the aprons with biscuits (see Biscuit Joinery on page 16) and/or fasten the aprons to the top with screws in oversize holes. This method is used for Move Over. Refer to pages 29-32 for a description of the procedure. For this table, use #10 biscuits and set the aprons in ¼" from the outside faces of the legs.

MAKING THE APRONS AND ASSEMBLING THE TABLE

1. Prepare maple or poplar stock ¾" thick and 2½" wide for the aprons (E). Cut the aprons to 13½" long.

2. Cut slots for the four table top fasteners on the inside faces of the aprons, one per apron. You may cut the slots with a biscuit joiner, or you may cut one long, ¼"-deep slot with the table saw. In either case, the slot must begin slightly more than the depth of the fastener from the top edge of the apron. Usually this distance is ⅜", but check your fasteners before cutting the slots. If you use a biscuit joiner, center the slot lengthwise on each apron. See figure 2 and photo 4.

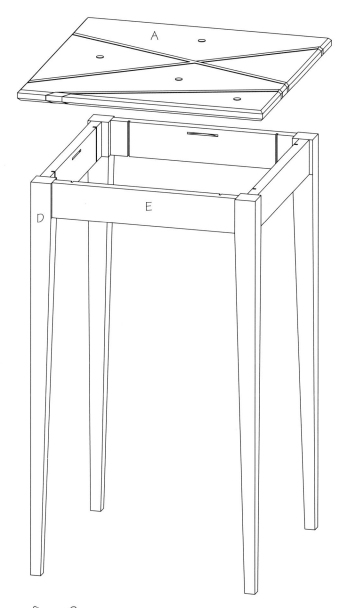

figure 2

3. The corner brackets require vertical slots on the inside faces of the aprons. Stand a leg upside down on a flat surface, and butt two aprons up to the inside faces of the leg. The outside faces of the leg should protrude ¼" from the outside faces of the aprons. Hold one of your brackets on top of the aprons so that its flanges are equidistant from the leg. Mark the aprons at the flanges (see photo 3).

4. With the table saw blade set ¼" high (or enough to accommodate the flanges on your brackets), set the rip fence a little farther from the blade than the

Photo 3

Photo 4

distance from your marks to the ends of the aprons. You will want to test this distance on scraps before cutting slots in your aprons. Use the miter gauge to maintain control of the apron, and place the end of the apron against the rip fence as you make your cut. Cut slots in two scraps. Test the rip fence setting by assembling the scraps with the leg and the bracket. You can keep using the same scraps to gradually arrive at a perfect fit. Then cut bracket slots in each end of all the aprons.

5. Assemble the legs, aprons, and brackets upside down on a flat surface. Mark the positions of all screw holes in the legs and aprons. Drill appropriate pilot holes at all those marks.

6. Sand the aprons to 220, easing the bottom corners.

7. Paint the legs and the aprons with black lacquer or send them out to be professionally finished.

8. Assemble the legs, aprons, and brackets upside down on a flat surface. Drive all necessary screws to attach the brackets to the aprons and to pull the legs into place.

9. Place the top (A) upside down on a padded surface. Position the base assembly upside down on the top, centering it both ways. Drill pilot holes for the table top fastener screws and drive them snug. Now all you have to do is decide in which area of the top your coffee cup looks best.

Glass Top Pedestal

DESIGNED BY RICHARD JUDD

With its boldly curved legs and glass top, this table adds drama to any room. Because of Judd's design capabilities, it is also easy to build. If you wish to use a clear finish instead of the black lacquer, you can use wenge for the legs and stretchers.

Materials

¼ **maple or poplar**

¼ **lacewood**

½" **x 14" diameter glass, pencil-polished edge**

Supplies

#10 x 2" pan head tapping screws

Cutting List

CODE	DESCRIPTION	QTY	MATERIAL	DIMENSIONS
A	Legs	4	poplar	¾" x 5" x 28"
B	Stretchers	2	poplar	¾" x 3" x 9"
C	Tenons	4	poplar	⅜" x 2¼" x 2⁷⁄₁₆"
D	Shelf	1	lacewood	¾" x 8¹⁵⁄₁₆" diameter

CUTTING THE JOINTS

1. Flatten, thickness, and joint one edge of stock for the legs (A) and the stretchers (B). (See Flattening, Thicknessing, and Jointing on page 8 to review this process.) Flatten and thickness (and joint and glue up, if necessary) lacewood stock for the shelf (D).

2. Rip and joint the stretcher stock to 3" wide.

3. Cut the legs (A) to a length of 28" using a drop stop. (Refer to Drop Stops, Jigs and Fixtures on page 12 for more information.) Cut the stretchers (B) to length as well.

4. The top end of each leg receives a ¾" high by 2½" deep notch (see figure 1). To do this on the table saw, raise the blade to 2½" high or slightly lower, and move the rip fence to ¾" from the far side of the blade. Use the miter gauge to push all four legs through the blade at once, with their top ends butted against the rip fence and their jointed edges down on the table. This minimizes tear-out next to the kerf. Set the rip fence to 2⁷⁄₁₆" from the far side of the blade. Use a scrap with a square end to push each leg through the blade, with the leg held vertically, and its jointed edge against the fence. The scrap might be a piece of ¾" plywood about 5" wide and long enough to push the leg all the way past the blade without getting your pushing hand too close to the blade. The pushing scrap helps control the leg as it goes past the blade and also pushes the cutoff away from the blade so that it doesn't come flying back at you.

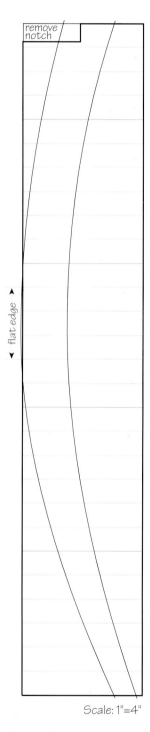

remove notch

flat edge

Scale: 1"=4"

Figure 1

5. Richard Judd uses loose tenons for the joints between the legs and stretchers, but you could use biscuits just as well. (See Biscuit Joinery on page 16 for a description of that method.) In these instructions, I will follow Richard's procedure. On the jointed edge of each leg, measure up from the bottom and mark the edge at 14⅜" and 16⅝". Cut 1¼"-deep mortises between those lines, centered thicknesswise. There's no need to square the ends of the mortises.

6. Cut centered mortises 2¼" wide and 1¼" deep in the ends of the stretchers.

7. The stretchers have a crosslap joint at their centers (see photo 1). Set the blade on your table saw to 1½" high. Set the drop stop on the miter gauge to 4⅜" from the near side of the blade. Cut through the two stretchers held together on edge and butted against the drop stop. Then turn the stretchers end-for-end, and make another cut right next to the first one. Move the drop stop ⅛" farther from the blade, and repeat the two cuts. You now have a ½"-wide dado in each stretcher. Move the drop stop outward little by little until you have a snug sliding fit between each dado and the thickness of the other stretcher.

8. With the stretchers lapped together, decide which will be their bottom edges. On the bottom edges (one has a dado and the other doesn't) mark in from the ends 1¾". Bore ⅜" countersinks centered on those marks to 1½" from the top edges (1½" deep). Drill a ¹¹⁄₆₄" hole from the center of each countersink through the top edge of its stretcher.

Photo 1

9. Sand the stretchers to 220 grit, but try not to loosen the crosslap joint by sanding too much. Ease the bottom corners with 220 sandpaper.

10. Thickness and rip stock for the loose tenons (C). Plane the stock to a sliding fit in the mortises. Before cutting them to length, round off the long corners with a block plane. Go ahead and check the fit of all the joints, as shown in photos 2 and 3. While the pieces are together, measure across from top notch to top notch (I couldn't resist) to make sure that the 14"-diameter top will fit. Then order the glass.

SHAPING THE LEGS AND SHELF

1. Following figure 1 (page 93), make a pattern for the legs from matte board or thin plywood. (See Fair Curves and Patterns on page 12 for helpful tips.) Notice that the area on the jointed edge of the legs from 14" to 17" from the floor must remain flat.

2. Trace the pattern onto the legs. The outside top corner will be 4" from the jointed edge, and the bottom corner will be 5" from the edge.

3. Band saw barely outside the lines. Clean up the saw marks with a low angle block plane and a spokeshave. Use the spokeshave at an angle to increase its effective base length. Try to produce fair curves, without humps and hollows, and keep the edges square to the faces of the legs. You can use a belt sander to finish smoothing the inside (convex) edges of the legs, but do not belt sand the outside curves. Embedded grit will quickly ruin your router bit in the next step.

Photo 2

4. With a ball bearing ⅜" radius cutter in the router table, round the outside corners of the legs. Sand all surfaces of the legs to 220 grit, except the flat joint area on the inside edge. Ease all the corners except in the joint area.

5. Working on its bottom side, draw a 9"-diameter circle on the stock for the shelf (D). Use a sharp pencil and band saw to the line, so that sanding the saw marks will reduce the diameter to 8¹⁵⁄₁₆". Sand all the surfaces of the shelf to 220 grit, and ease the corners.

ASSEMBLING AND FINISHING

1. Remember that the countersinks are on the bottom edges of the stretchers. Glue inside the mortises of one stretcher and its two legs. Push in the tenons and clamp the joints closed. Immediately stand the legs on a flat surface and measure from the "floor" to the bottom of the stretcher at both of its ends: it should be 14" from the floor. Adjust the position of the stretcher by loosening the clamp and judiciously applying a deadblow hammer. Use a straightedge to make sure that all three pieces lie in the same plane. Assemble the other stretcher and two legs in the same way.

2. Sand the areas around the joints to 220 grit. Slide the crosslap joint together. The top edges of the stretchers should be flush and the legs should all touch the floor. Take the two pieces apart for finishing.

3. Richard Judd finishes the legs and stretchers with black lacquer and the shelf with clear lacquer. You may do this yourself or send them out to a professional finisher. If you used a dark wood for the legs and stretchers, try the burnished oil finish described on page 20.

4. When finishing is complete, reassemble the crosslap joint and put the shelf in place. The grain of the shelf should run diagonally to the stretchers. Use a skinny awl or a long finishing nail to mark the locations for the screws. Mark or remember how the shelf sits on the stretchers. Drill ⅛" holes ½" deep at the marks. Put the shelf back in place and fasten the parts together with four #10 x 2" screws. Isn't that elegant? Oh yeah: drop the glass top in the notches.

Figure 2

Photo 3

Four-Square Table

DESIGNED BY JOHN BICKEL

This handsome table defies its rather heavy dimensions by breaking up its masses into several sections. The thin edge of its top seems to hover above the temple space below. It is relatively easy to build and complements many contemporary interiors.

Materials

¾" plywood veneered with madrone burl

¾" plywood

4/4 wenge

8/4 wenge

Supplies

#0 biscuits

#6 x 2" drywall screws

#6 x 1¼" drywall screws

Cutting List

CODE	DESCRIPTION	QTY	MATERIAL	DIMENSIONS
A	Top Center	1	plywood with madrone burl veneer	¾" x 20½" x 20½"
B	Top Edges	4	4/4 wenge	¾" x 1¾" x 24"
C	Base Center	1	plywood with madrone burl veneer	¾" x 12½" x 12½"
D	Base Edges	4	4/4 wenge	¾" x 2-¼" x 14"
E	Feet	4	4/4 wenge	⅜" x 2¼" x 2¼"
F	Legs	4	8/4 wenge	1¾" x 1¾" x 15⅞"
G	Subtop	1	plywood	¾" x 14" x 14"

MAKING THE TOP

1. Either purchase plywood with a suitable face veneer or veneer a piece of ¾" plywood with madrone burl. A 2' x 3' piece will be sufficient for the top center (A) and the base center (C). Remember to veneer both faces for stability. (Refer to Simple Veneering on page 18 for help.)

2. Cut a 20½" square from the veneered plywood.

3. Flatten, thickness, and joint enough stock for the top edges (B). (Refer to Flattening, Thicknessing, and Jointing on page 8.) Rip and joint the pieces to 1¾" wide.

4. Using a table saw or miter box, miter the ends of the top edges (B) to fit around the top center (A). See figure 1. Work your way around the top, fitting each

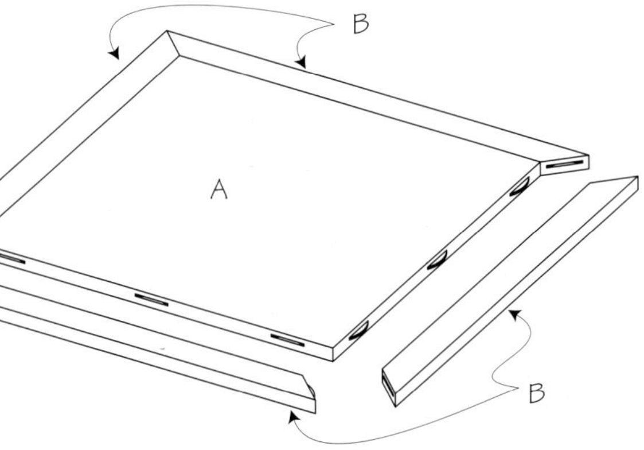

Figure 1

joint in turn. If you end up with a nice square frame just a little bit too small, adjust the size of the top center. If one of the top edges comes up a little short, joint its inside edge to effectively lengthen it.

5. Because gluing mitered edges around a panel can require about five hands, biscuits in all the joints will aid assembly and add a little strength to the joints. (Refer to Biscuit Joinery on page 16.) Using the tops of all pieces as the indexing surface, mark out and cut three #0 slots in each edge of the top center (A), matching slots in the inside edge of each top edge (B), and matching slots in the mitered ends of the edge pieces.

6. Do a trial assembly of the top center and the top edges, with all biscuits, clamps, and clamp pads in place. Disassemble the top, keeping everything in order—there will be no time for thinking or finding

once you begin to glue up. Consider using epoxy for a more leisurely glue-up (see Structural Epoxy on page 19.) Glue biscuits in the top center first, then in the right-hand end of each top edge. Apply glue to the inside edge, the left-hand mitered end, and the slots of all four top edges. Push one top edge into place against its edge of the top center, carefully but quickly aligning the corners. Then push on the opposite top edge, across the top center from the first. Push the remaining top edges into place and quickly begin clamping. Clamp first across the first two edges you applied, then clamp as necessary. If you skipped the dry assembly, you're paying for your laziness now, aren't you? Take a break to consider alternatives to miter joints.

7. Scrape or sand off the glue on the top and bottom of the top assembly.

8. Put a rip blade on the table saw. Set the blade angle of the table saw to 25°. Set the rip fence, with a tall face, ¼" from the blade. Bevel the edges of the top assembly with the assembly on edge, its face against the fence. Feed just fast enough to keep the wood from burning (see figure 2).

9. Sand the top assembly. Begin with a belt sander on the beveled faces of the top edges (B). A random-orbit sander will work well for the top surface, but make very sure to remove all scratches left by the previous grit with the next grit. You will have to hand sand with your last and finest grit to remove swirls left by the jitterbug. Ease all the corners slightly with the last paper you use.

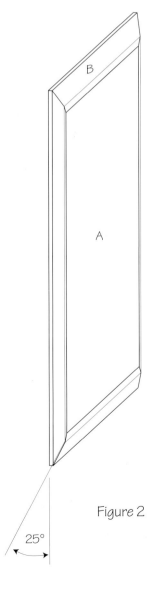

Figure 2

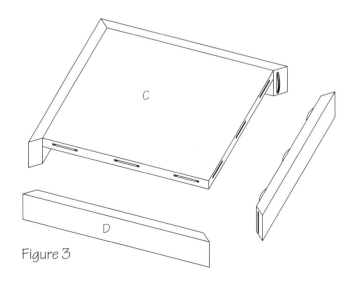

Figure 3

MAKING THE BASE

1. Assembling the base is just like making the top, except that the edge pieces are oriented vertically instead of horizontally. Cut a 12½" square from the remaining veneered plywood for the base center (C).

2. Flatten, thickness, joint, and rip stock for the base edges (D). You'll need four pieces ¾" x 2¼" and more than 14" long. Make an extra piece now for insurance and to cut up for feet (E).

3. Cut the mitered ends of the base edges (D) across the inside face. See figure 3. You'll probably want to use the table saw with its miter gauge set square and the blade angled 45°. Work around the base center (C) as before. Mark the positions of the base edges.

4. Cut three #0 biscuit slots in each edge of the base center (C) and matching slots in the inside faces of the base edges (D). Set the front plate of your biscuit joiner to 45° to cut slots in the mitered ends of the base edges.

5. Follow the same procedure as you did for assembling the top to dry-fit, glue, and clamp the base edges (D) to the base center (C). You'll need at least one clamp each way across the top surface and four clamps around the bottoms of the base edges. You

may be able to use a band clamp with corner protectors around the bottom instead of the four clamps, but be sure to have an extra bar clamp ready for adjustments.

6. Sand the base assembly as you did the top assembly.

7. Plane the extra piece from Step 2 to ⅜" thick. Cut four 2¼" lengths to make the feet (E).

8. Sand one face, one edge, and one end of each foot. Ease the corners. Then glue a foot to the bottom of each corner of the base assembly, so that the foot protrudes ¼" on each side. See figure 4.

MAKING THE LEGS AND ASSEMBLING THE TABLE

1. Mill ¾ wenge to size for the legs (F). You'll need four pieces, each 1¾" x 1¾" x 15⅞". Cut them to length.

2. Sand the faces of the legs and ease the long corners.

3. Cut the subtop (G) from ¾" plywood, 14" square. Sand one face and all edges.

4. On the top surface of the base assembly and the sanded surface of the subtop (G), lightly pencil a line 3" from each edge, forming a centered, 8" square. The legs (F) will be installed inside the corners of those squares. Use a cut-off from the leg stock to trace the positions of the tops and bottoms of the legs. With a straightedge aligned with diagonal corners of the base assembly, draw a line diagonally across each leg position. Do the same on the subtop.

5. Within each leg position on the base assembly and the subtop (G), drill two ⁵⁄₆₄" holes through the plywood, each on the diagonal line and about ⅝" from a corner. On the top (unsanded) surface of the subtop, cut shallow ⅜" countersinks for screw heads in all eight of the holes.

6. Next comes the tricky part: holding each leg in position while you drill a pilot hole through each hole in the subtop. Here's one way: Clamp the subtop in your bench vise with its good face toward the bench. Lay a leg on the bench with its top end against the subtop. Then open the vise slightly so that you can position the subtop precisely relative to the leg. Clamp the leg in place while leaving room to drill a ⁵⁄₃₂" pilot hole into the end of the leg, using the hole in the subtop as a guide. Mark the leg and the subtop to key its position. Then go on to the next leg.

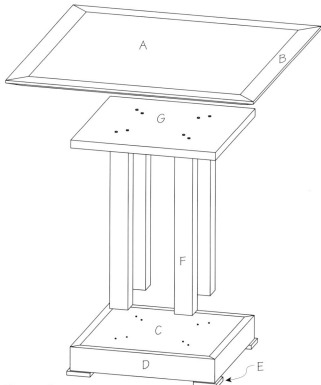

Figure 4

7. Once you have a pilot hole in the top of each leg, drive #6 x 2" screws to secure the legs to the subtop. Make sure that each leg is properly positioned, drill ⁵⁄₃₂" pilot holes through the remaining four holes in the subtop, and drive four more 2" screws.

8. Place the subtop top down on the bench, so that the legs are sticking upward. Put the base assembly face down on the legs, aligning at least one leg with its marked square. If you have a large enough bar clamp, clamp that leg in place against the base assembly. Otherwise, just hold the base assembly firmly while you drill the first pilot hole. Drive a screw through that hole, then go on to the next leg. When all four legs are secured to the base assembly, set the whole thing on the subtop, and drill the last four holes.

9. Now remove all the screws holding the legs, marking the positions of the legs within the squares on the base assembly and the subtop and on the ends of the legs. Use numbers 1 through 8 and an arrow in each case to show orientation. Then erase and sand off any pencil marks which will not be covered by the leg ends.

10. Completely finish all parts of the table. See Burnished Oil Finish on page 20 for one option.

11. Reassemble the table by attaching the legs to the base assembly and then to the subtop. Finally, place the top assembly, upside down, on a towel or a piece of foam. Center the subtop on the top assembly. Countersink and drill clearance holes with a ⁹⁄₆₄" bit through the subtop, two on each side about ¾" in from the edge. Then drill ⁵⁄₃₂" pilot holes no deeper than ½" into the bottom of the top center. Before driving any screws, remove the subtop/legs/base assembly and clear away all drilling dust. Reposition the subtop and drive #6 x 1¼" screws into the eight holes in the top center. You're finished, except for turning the table over and carrying it into the house.

Open Grid Table

DESIGNED BY RON TRUMBLE

In designing this table, Ron Trumble had in mind the perforated quality of a windowed wall. In addition to providing an interesting decorative element, the open grid reminds us that a table's purpose is to hold things off the floor, not to catch spills. Trumble makes the impressive joinery in the top accessible with a few clever jigs.

Materials

4/4 wenge

3/4" birdseye maple-veneered MDF or plywood

4/4 maple

8/4 maple

Supplies

Cyanoacrylate glue

#20 biscuits

#6 x 1¼" drywall screws

#6 x 1½" pan head screws

Cutting List

CODE	DESCRIPTION	QTY	MATERIAL	DIMENSIONS
A	Grid Strips	8	wenge	¼" x 13/16" x 4"
B	Top Panel	1	MDF with birdseye maple veneer	¾" x 14" x 14"
C	Top Borders	4	maple	¾" x 3" x 20"
D	Legs	4	maple	1¾" x 1¾" x 19¼"
E	Aprons	4	maple	¾" x 3" x 14"
F	Corner Braces	4	maple	⅞" x 3" x 3½"

MAKING THE GRID

1. Flatten, thickness to 13/16", and joint one edge of a small piece of 4/4 wenge. The piece must be long enough not to cause problems for your planer, but only needs to contain 32" of ¼" widths in 4" increments. In other words, a piece 17" long and 2" wide would be plenty. (Still, since these pieces are small and delicate, a prudent worker will make extras.)

2. Rip a strip 9/32" wide on the table saw. Joint the edge, and rip another strip. Repeat until you have enough strips. Do not thickness the strips yet!

3. Using a dado blade on the table saw, cut a ¼" slot about ⅜" deep near one end of two strips. Use these slots as gauges as you thickness and sand the strips to

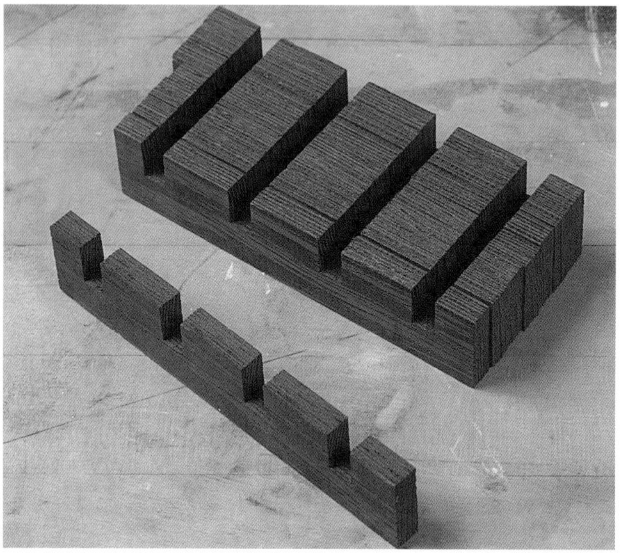

Photo 1

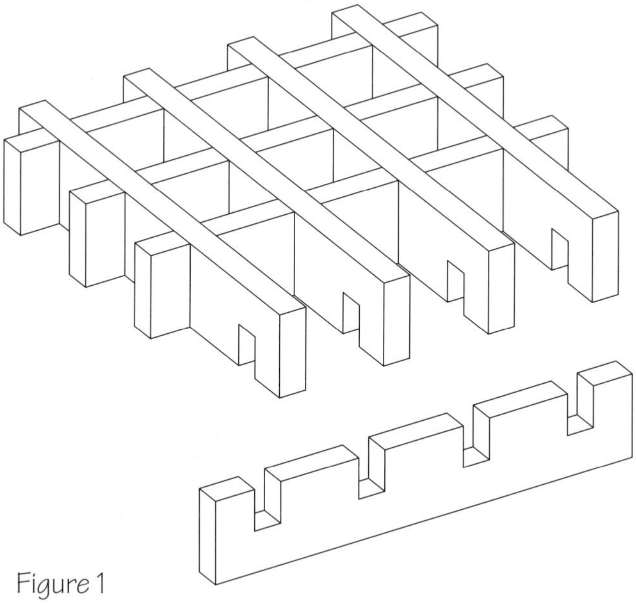

Figure 1

the width of the slot. This way you can achieve a sliding fit with no slop.

4. Switch to a good crosscut blade on the table saw, and use a drop stop to cut at least eight grid strips (A) 4" long (see Drop Stops, Jigs, and Fixtures on page 12).

5. Put the ¼" dado blade back on the table saw. To make a grid with 3/4" square openings and ⅜" stubs on the outside, you need to cut slots halfway through the grid strips (A), ⅜" and 1-⅜" from each end. First, set the height of the dado blade to a little over ⅜". Cut a slot in each of two extra or cut-off strips. Slide the two slots together. Adjust the height of the dado blade until the test strips go together a little past flush. A very little.

6. Clamp a piece of hardwood to the fence of your miter gauge, extending past the dado blade, to reduce tear-out. Clamp a stop to the hardwood so that its face is exactly 3⅜" from the near corner of the teeth of the dado blade. Cut a slot through the thickness of both ends of all the grid strips. Those slots are ⅜" from the ends of the strips, aren't they?

7. Clamp the stop 2⅜" from the blade and cut two more slots in each grid strip. Your strips now look like those in photo 1.

8. Apply a small drop of cyanoacrylate glue to the bottom of each slot in eight grid strips. Assemble the grid quickly and allow the glue to cure (see figure 1).

9. Use a band saw or a hand saw to cut the stubs from the grid (see photo 2). Sand the edges smooth, but be sure to keep them flat and square.

MAKING THE TOP

1. Veneer a piece of ¾" MDF larger than 14" square with birdseye maple veneer. (See Simple Veneering on page 18 for help.) Trim the veneered MDF to 14" square for the top panel (B) by cutting two adjacent sides absolutely square. Then use the rip fence set at 14" from the blade to cut the other two sides.

2. Find some scrap ¾" MDF or plywood to make a jig to cut the hole for the grid in the top panel. Use the grid to set your rip fence to cut a strip of MDF about 26" long and the exact width of the grid. From that strip cut two 10" pieces and two pieces 3" or longer. Edge glue these pieces together around, but not to, the grid. Figure 2 shows the arrangement of the jig pieces and photo 3 shows the completed jig. Remove

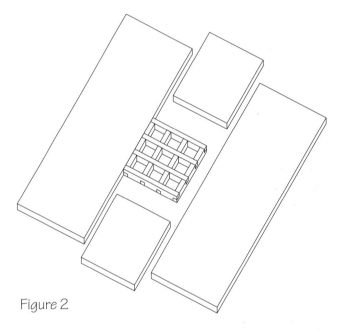

Figure 2

Photo 2

Photo 3

the grid as soon as the pieces are clamped. When the glue has cured, sand the jig to flatten it and to remove excess glue.

3. Center the opening of the jig on the top panel (B) with the help of pencil lines drawn diagonally from corner to corner. Trace the opening. Remove most of the material inside the opening by drilling a series of large, overlapping holes, or by drilling one hole from which to cut out waste with a saber saw. In any case, stay ⅛" inside the traced line.

Photo 4

Photo 5

4. Put the jig on the top panel again, matching the corners of the jig opening to the diagonal lines on the panel. Clamp the pieces together. Use a ball-bearing-guided, flush trimming bit in your router to expand the opening in the top panel to the dimensions of the grid. Photo 4 shows the jig being removed after trimming the opening.

5. Square the corners of the opening with a sharp mortise chisel (photo 5). Begin cutting from the bottom side of the panel, and cut only half-way through. Then cut from the top, leaving a little bit to be carefully trimmed with a wide paring chisel (photo 6). Try the grid in the opening to make sure it fits.

6. Apply glue inside the opening, and push the grid in from the top side of the panel (photo 7). Push and tap until the top of the grid is flush with the top of the panel—it must not go beneath the level of the veneer. Sand the bottom of the grid flush with the panel.

7. Flatten, thickness, and joint one edge of maple boards for the top borders (C) (see Flattening, Thicknessing, and Jointing on page 8 for a refresher course). You may as well prepare stock for the aprons (E) and the corner braces (F) at the same time, since their thicknesses and widths are the same as those of the borders. Rip the material to just over 3", and clean up the new edge with one pass over the jointer.

8. Miter the ends of the top borders very carefully, matching each border to a particular side of the top panel and marking them. Before cutting any aprons to

Photo 6

length, make sure that you are cutting 45° accurately by cutting a miter on one end each of two pieces of border. Hold these against a corner of the top panel to look for gaps in the miter joint. Adjust your setup as necessary, and try again. When your angles are accurate, mark and cut the borders to length. If you happen to cut one short, remember that jointing its inside edge will effectively lengthen that edge, giving you another chance.

9. With the borders laid out around the panel, mark across the joints for the biscuit jointer (see Biscuit Joinery on page 16 for help). Mark the middle of each miter joint, and mark 3" in from each panel corner along the edge joints. Set the biscuit jointer fence to ⅜" and cut slots for #20 biscuits at every mark (see figure 3).

10. Make sure you have clamps, pads, biscuits, glue, and a pure heart before you begin assembling the top. You must work quickly and accurately throughout this process. Lay out the top panel and the top borders in their relative positions. Glue and push biscuits into all the slots in the top panel first. Then glue and biscuit the left end of each border (you decide which is which). Glue the slots and edges of each border in turn and push it into place. Make sure to get each one positioned accurately as you go—those biscuits puff up quickly. Because of that, Ron Trumble suggests positioning two opposite aprons first, clamping them, and then pushing the other two into place. After you clamp across the top, check for

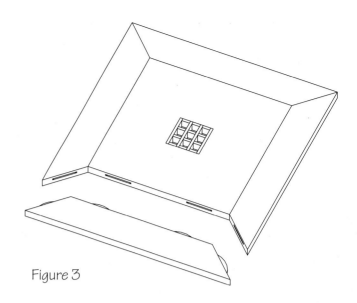

Figure 3

flatness with a straightedge across all the joints. Adjust the clamp positions to correct any misalignment.

11. Scrape off excess glue, and sand the completed top to 220 grit or finer. You will, of course, avoid sanding through the veneer. Ease the corners around the edge.

MAKING THE LEGS AND APRONS

1. Prepare maple stock for the legs (D), and cut the legs to length using the drop stop on your table saw (see Drop Stops, Jigs, and Fixtures on page 12).

2. These "bell-bottom" legs taper from 1" square at the top to 1¾" square at the bottom. Their inside faces remain vertical. Refer to figure 4. Make a simple tapering jig from scrap plywood, such as that pictured and described on page 80. On a piece of plywood about 4" wide and 21" long, measure in from one edge 1¾" and mark at one end. Beginning 19¼" from that end, mark 1" from the same edge. Lay a framing square on the plywood with its long arm aligned with the first mark, its corner at the second mark and its short arm toward the near edge (1" away). Trace around the square, and cut to the line with the band saw. Taper two sides of each leg with this jig.

3. Using the drop stop, cut the aprons (E) to 14" long. Mark their good faces.

4. If your biscuit jointer doesn't have guide lines 1½" each side of the centerline, mark them on the top of the base near the cutter face. Use the biscuit jointer without its fence, its base flat on the bench. Hold or

Photo 7

clamp each apron, good face up, on the bench as well. Cut slots for #20 biscuits, centered in the ends of the aprons.

5. To cut slots in the legs, place a ⅛" plywood spacer between the jointer base and the bench, while holding each leg on the bench surface, one square face down and one toward the jointer (see photo 8). Align one of the 1½" marks on the jointer with the top of the leg and cut into the inside face. Twist and flip each leg to cut its second slot.

6. Mark the inside of each apron at points 3" in from each end and 1¼" from the top edge. Tilt the table on your drill press 20°, and attach a fence which will hold the aprons while you drill from the marked points through the top edge. Start each hole with a ⅜" forstner bit, and stop 1" from the top edge, at a point where you have a shoulder for the screw head to bear against (see photo 9). From the center of that hole, drill through the top edge with a bit sized to the outside diameter of your screw threads (⅛" for a #6 screw).

7. Sand the legs and the aprons to 220 grit, and ease the long-grain corners. Keep the joint area of the legs flat.

ASSEMBLY AND FINISHING

1. Tilt the blade of your table saw to 45°, and use a drop stop to cut the mitered ends of the corner braces (F). They are mitered across their thickness, as shown in figure 4.

Photo 8

2. Gather your clamps, pads, #20 biscuits, glue, legs, and aprons. Put plastic on the bench and a record on the Victrola. Or not. Arrange the legs and aprons as they will go together. Apply glue to the slots in each leg and add biscuits. Add glue to the slots in one apron, and add its two legs. Make sure that the top edge of the apron is flush with the tops of the legs. Clamp that side, then assemble the opposite side of the base in the same way. Glue the slots in the remaining aprons, and clamp the base together. Check to see that the joints are uniformly closed. Use a ruler to measure the diagonals at the tops of the legs to make sure that the base is square. Adjust the clamps as necessary.

3. When the glue has dried, apply glue to the miters of the corner braces, and clamp them in place, flush with the top edges of the aprons. Spring clamps near the ends of the braces work well. Don't pull the base out of square with your clamps. Check the diagonals again to see that you haven't.

4. Use a tapered countersink with a ⅜₂" bit to drill pilot holes across the miter joints of the braces and into the aprons. Two holes through each joint, ¾" from the top and bottom, will be plenty. Drive #6 x 1¼" drywall screws into the holes.

5. You can lacquer your table, as Ron Trumble does, or try the burnished oil finish described on page 20, or use another clear finish.

6. Place the top, upside down, on a padded surface. Center the base on the top. Use a finishing nail through the angled holes in the aprons to mark for pilot holes. Drill ⅜₂" holes only ¼" deep or so at the marks. Screw the base to the top using 1½" pan head screws.

Photo 9

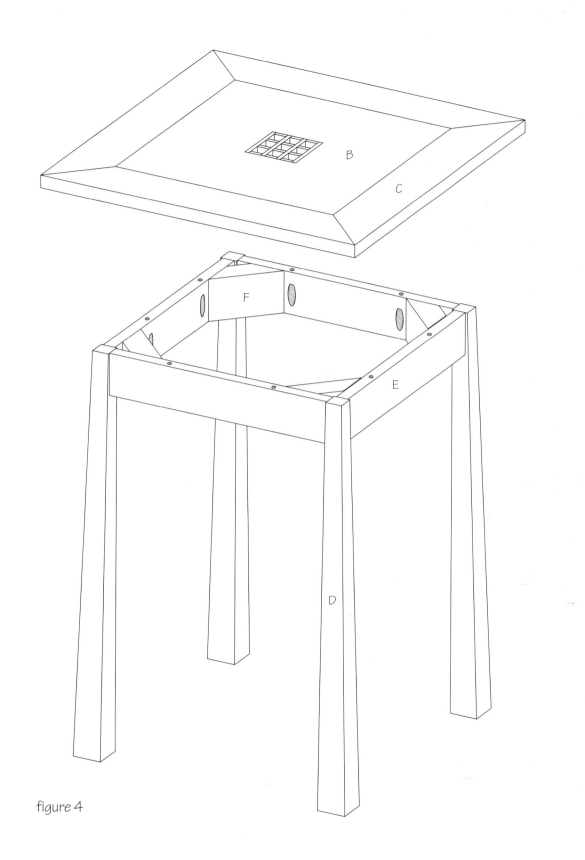

figure 4

Triangle Plant Stand

DESIGNED BY JOHN BICKEL

This plant stand was designed to match the Bickels' house, which has a triangular footprint. Its updated Arts and Crafts style will complement many interiors, and its construction will be a healthy challenge to many builders. Here's a chance to learn about fixtures and guides!

Materials

4/4 cherry

6/4 cherry

4/4 walnut

3/4" MDF

Madrone burl veneer

Supplies

1/4" dowel

3/8" dowel

Cutting List

CODE	DESCRIPTION	QTY	MATERIAL	DIMENSIONS
A	Top Shelf	1	walnut	7/8" x 11½" x 13½"
B	Inner Shelves	3	walnut	½" x 5½" x 6½"
C	Outer Posts	3	cherry	1¼" x 1 7/16" x 33⅜"
D	Inner Posts	3	cherry	1¼" x 1 7/16" x 27½"
E	Base Layers	3	MDF	¾" x 13½" x 15½"
F	Base Edges	3	cherry	⅛" x 2¼" x 16"
G	Feet	3	walnut	⅜" x 2" x 2½"

CUTTING THE SHELVES

1. Flatten and thickness walnut for the top shelf (A), the inner shelves (B), and the feet (G). (See Flattening, Thicknessing, and Jointing on page 8 to review this process.) Keep in mind that these pieces are all triangles, so you will not need as much wood as simply tripling the length measurements above would suggest. If you glue the top shelf from two pieces 6" wide, you will need a board no more than 21" long. The inner shelves require a board 14" long, and the feet can be made from the shortest length your planer will take (or resaw a shelf scrap on the table saw). Joint one edge of each of your boards and rip each to the greatest width it will produce.

2. Cut the board for the top shelf (A) into pieces that will produce an equilateral triangle 13½" on a side (see figure 1). Arrange the pieces of the top shelf, and joint their gluing edges. (See Gluing Table Tops on page 10 for helpful tips.) Center the shorter piece on the edge of the longer piece, and mark its position. Glue the edge of the shorter piece, and clamp the shelf with a double pipe clamp, or two or three alternated single clamps.

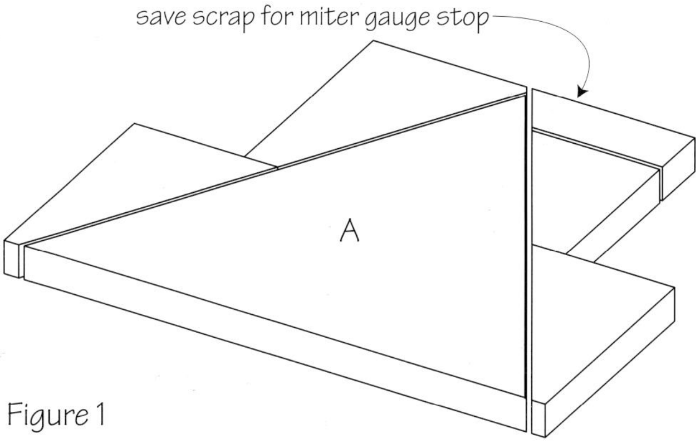

save scrap for miter gauge stop
A

Figure 1

3. When the glue has cured, belt sand the top shelf flat. Find the center of the long edge of the shelf blank. Square across to the opposite edge, and mark the beginning of the first saw cut. (Here's a free tip: Cut a sheet of 300 or 400 grit wet-or-dry sandpaper into strips as wide as your miter gauge fence is high. Use contact cement to glue them—rough side out, of course—to your fence. You'll now have less trouble controlling angled cuts. Simple and cost-effective, like reading this tip.) Set the miter gauge on the table saw to 30°, with the blade end of the fence closer to you. Cut one side of the shelf, holding the workpiece firmly to resist its efforts to slide closer to the saw blade.

4. Rip a 1½" strip from the longer edge of the cut-off scrap you just made (see figure 1). (Keep the rest of the scrap, too.) Use this strip as a stop for cutting the rest of the triangular shelves and feet in this project. Clamp the strip to the miter guide fence, forming a notch for the top shelf's corner, 13½" from the blade. Use a thin, metal ruler for this measurement. Slide the top shelf into the notch and cut its third side.

5. Remove the strip, and cut close to the end of the board for the three inner shelves (B). Replace the strip, clamping it 6½" from the blade. Flip the board, fitting its acute corner into the notch, and cut the first inner shelf. Flip and cut twice more to produce the rest of the shelves. Save one of the scrap pieces.

6. If you haven't done so, prepare a piece of walnut ⅜" x 2" x 6" (or longer) for the feet. After the first cut, clamp the notch strip 2½" from the blade. Cut the three feet, being careful to keep your fingers clear of the blade.

7. Adjust the miter gauge so that the end of the fence nearer the blade is away from you and set to 30°. To cut the corners from the shelves, clamp the notch strip 1⅛" closer to the blade than its previous setting: 12⅜" for the top shelf and 5⅜" for the inner shelves (see figure 2). You want the resulting truncated corner to measure exactly 1⅛", so you should prudently measure all 12 shelf edges to find out how much they vary. There's no need to recut the shelves. Simply begin with the largest edge against your fence and adjust the notch strip as you go. Cut off those corners now. Measure each one as soon as you cut it, and cut a little more if necessary. It would be a very good thing to avoid cutting off too much with the first cut. But that's woodworking, isn't it?

8. Sand the faces and the long edges of the shelves and feet to 220 grit. Ease the long corners but not those of the cut-off corners.

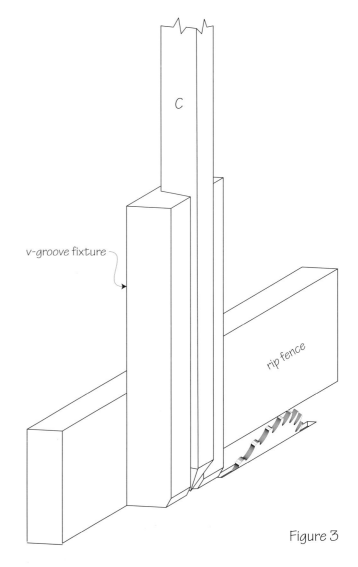

Figure 3

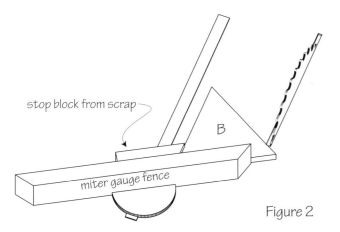

Figure 2

MAKING THE POSTS

1. The six posts are long and skinny, with the most obvious ones all but unsupported. If your cherry is not well-seasoned and comfortable with itself, these sticks may become warped as soon as they are released from the board. Therefore, it would be a good idea to allow for extra posts, in case some of them emerge too crooked. All six posts (C and D) can be cut, believe it or not, from a 6"-wide board 1¼" thick, so begin with a board 9" wide or two narrower ones. Flatten and thickness a piece of cherry at least 36" long, and joint one edge.

2. Tilt the blade of your table saw to 30°. With its jointed edge against the rip fence, on the side away from the top of the blade, rip the board as wide as possible. Flip the board end-for-end. Move the rip fence until the far side of the blade lines up with the 120° corner on top of the board. Check this by sighting down the board or by using a straightedge held even with the corner and extended to the blade. Cut into the board until the blade begins to clear the top face of the board. If the kerf is completely in the face of the board, but at the corner, keep on ripping. If not, back off and adjust the fence. Don't worry about the resulting stepped cut—that's why you're sawing a board which is longer than necessary.

3. Keep flipping and adjusting and ripping until you have six pretty-straight posts.

4. The tops of the outer posts (C) end in a pyramid. The extended angle between the side of the post and the face of the pyramid is 60°, and cutting this angle requires a fixture to hold the post steady and correctly angled. Make the fixture from a piece of wood at least 1¼" thick, about 5" wide and maybe 8" long. It must have parallel edges and one end cut square to the edges. Lower the table saw blade, still angled to 30°, until its top tooth is 1" off the table. Set the rip fence, still on the "open" side of the blade, to one-half the width of your fixture from the fence to the near side of the top tooth. Then move the fence ½₂" closer to the blade. Rip through the fixture piece twice to make a triangular groove.

5. Refer to figure 3, which represents the fixture ready for use (your blade may tilt the opposite direction). Place the fixture against the fence, groove out, and hold an outer post snugly in the groove. Set the fence so that the near side of the blade at the table is ⅜" from the outside face of the post. (You will be cut-

ting away the bottom corner of the fixture.) This cut will be too small to produce a point on the pyramid, but cut around the post at this setting to see how much to move the fence. Before each cut, clamp the post firmly in the groove. During the cut, hold the fixture squarely on the table, and the whole business tight against the fence. When you turn the post, make sure its point rests on the saw table and not in the saw slot. Move the fence closer to the blade until you cut a point that still touches the saw table. The corners between the post faces and the pyramid faces should meet at the corners of the post. Then cut the other two outer posts, which should require no further adjustments.

Whew. Take a break. You've done well, my friend. I'd tell you to throw that fixture away right now, but if you did, one of the posts would surely get stepped on and break within the next half-hour. So keep it around and look fondly upon it from time to time. Heck, you may even find another use for it later.

6. Return your table saw to its normal, everything-squared-up state. Set your drop stop to 33⅜" and cut the bottom ends of the outer posts. Hold one face of the post against the miter gauge, not against the table. (See Drop Stops Jigs, and Fixtures on page 12 to review.) Save one of those cut-off ends.

7. Use the drop stop to cut the inner posts 27½" long.

8. Finally, plane each corner of every post until you produce a ³⁄₁₆"-wide flat instead of the sharp corner (see figure 4).

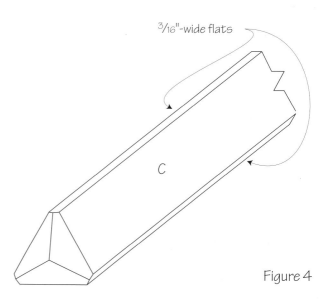

³⁄₁₆"-wide flats

C

Figure 4

MAKING THE BASE

1. Cut three equilateral triangles, 16" on a side, from ¾" MDF. By this time you should know how to do that, but note that these triangles are oversize to allow for trimming. Veneer one side of one triangle with madrone burl. That piece will be the top layer of the base. Glue the three base layers (E) into a stack with the veneer on top.

2. Trim the stack to size by cutting only enough from one side to make the layers even. Put that sawn edge against the miter gauge to cut the second side only enough to clean it up. Use your notch stop set 15½" from the blade to cut the third side.

3. Mill a piece of ¼ cherry to 2⅜" wide, 18" long, and as thick as can be for the base edges (F). Resaw this piece on the table saw with a sharp ripping blade. Saw a ⅛"-thick slice from one face, and plane the sawn face of the blank before sawing a slice from each face of the thinner blank. That way, each ⅛" slice has a planed face to glue to the edge of the base layers. The saw blade can glaze the surface of the wood, which inhibits adhesion.

4. Glue one base edge, planed face in, to an edge of the base stack. If you have a slightly warped piece of wood around, now is the time to use it as a clamping pad. Put the concave side against the cherry to distribute the clamping pressure. Clamp the edge with a bar clamp, its fixed face on the fixture you saved from cutting the ends of the posts. Keep the fixture/clamping pad away from the veneered top surface of the stack to avoid damaging the top corner. Didn't I tell you it would be a mistake to throw that fixture away?

5. When the glue has cured, trim the ends of the first base edge (F), using a fine-toothed hand saw, such as a dozuki saw. Hold the blade against the edge of the stack with your free hand to guide your cut. Use 150-grit sandpaper on a block to clean up the ends and make them flush with the other sides of the stack. Take great care to avoid rounding the corners. Repeat steps 4 and 5 to glue the other two base edges in place.

6. Use a low angle block plane to trim the bottoms of the edges flush with the bottom of the base. Be careful around the corners. Plane the top edges close to the veneer, but don't touch the veneer. Sand the base to 220 grit, making the tops of the edges flush with the veneer in the process. Ease all the corners.

7. Glue the feet (G) to the base so that ¼" of foot sticks out on both sides of each corner.

MAKING THE JOINTS

1. From the scrap end of post material you saved, cut a ½"-thick piece. Use the scraps from the top shelf and the inner shelf to cut ½"-wide and 1⅛"-long pieces, leaving their thicknesses as is. These three little chunks will serve for dowelling guides to make all the joints for this stand.

2. Make sure that the table of your drill press is square to the chuck. Drill a ¼" hole, centered on what would be the edge of the shelves, through the two shelf guides. Drill a ⅜" hole through the post guide, centered in the triangle.

3. On the top side of each of the shelf guides (that is, the top side if each were still part of its shelf), draw an arrow pointing toward one of the drilled faces. Label the arrow "S" for "shelf." On a triangular end of the post guide, draw an arrow toward one of its faces. Then turn it over and draw another arrow toward the same face. Mark one side "T" for "top," and mark the other side "B" for "bottom," or "base," or "below," or "be done, already." (See figure 5.)

4. Mark the top faces of all four shelves.

5. Center the top shelf (A), top upwards, on the base, and clamp it. Hold the post guide against a corner of the shelf, arrow pointed at the shelf and

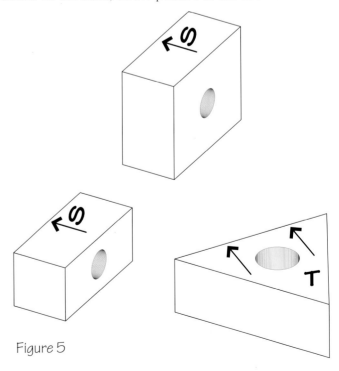

Figure 5

112

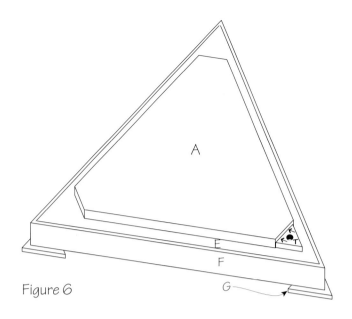

Figure 6

9. On one face of each of the inner posts (D), measure down from the top and mark 7½", 10", and 12½". Clamp an inner post in the fixture, marked face up. Place the clamp above the top mark. On top of that post, spring-clamp another inner post so that its end lands on the 12½" mark. Hold the inner shelf guide against the two posts, arrow showing and pointed upward. Drill a ¼" hole as before. Repeat this procedure at all the marks on all the inner posts.

10. Clamp the top shelf (A), top up, to your bench so that one corner is near the edge of the bench. Hold the top shelf guide, arrow up and toward the shelf, centered against that corner. Drill a ¼" hole 1" deep through the guide. Do the same at the other two corners of the top shelf.

11. Repeat the procedure in step 9 at each corner of the inner shelves (B), using the inner shelf guide, of course.

12. Switch back to the ⅜" bit. Clamp a post, shelf side up, in the v-groove fixture, near the edge of your bench, so that the bottom end of the post faces you. Leave a little of the fixture showing to provide support for the post guide. Hold the post guide against the end of the post, with "B" showing and the arrow pointing up. Drill at least 1" into the post. Repeat this procedure on the bottom ends of the outer posts (C) and both ends of the inner posts (D).

"T" showing. Drill a ⅜" hole at least 1" deep into the base, through the guide hole (see figure 6). Repeat at the other two corners.

6. Center an inner shelf (B), top upwards, on the base, and clamp it. Drill dowel holes at its corners, as you did in step 5.

7. Place the top shelf (A) upside down on a pad on your bench. Center an inner shelf (B), also upside down, on the top shelf, and clamp it. Drill dowel holes ⅝" deep at its corners as before.

8. Clamp one of the outer posts (C), in the v-groove fixture, to your bench top. Clamp about 3" from the top of the post. Align one end of an inner post (D) with the bottom of the outer post. Hold the two posts together with two spring clamps. Place the top shelf guide against the top of the inner post, arrow visible and pointing away from the outer post. Hold the guide firmly centered on the post as you drill a ¼" hole ¾" deep (but no more) into the post. (Figure 7 shows the arrangement of the pieces without the clamps.) Repeat this process on the other two outer posts.

FINISHING AND ASSEMBLY

1. After checking to see that all the pieces have been sanded, finish them completely with the burnished oil finish, described on page 20, or another clear finish. Try to leave the dowel holes free of oil and wax.

2. Cut ¼" and ⅜" dowels to size for all the joints. Chamfering the ends of the dowels will help them slide into their holes. Make three 6"-long v-blocks to facilitate clamping the posts to the shelves.

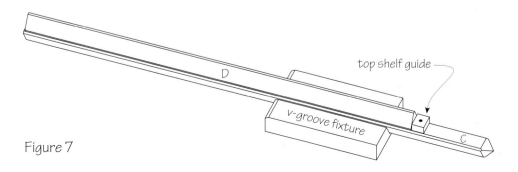

Figure 7

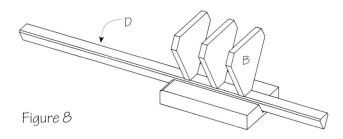

Figure 8

3. Proceed at each joint by putting a little glue all around inside the lip of a hole, dipping the dowel end in a puddle of glue, inserting the dowel, gluing the other hole and the other end of the dowel, and pushing the second piece into place. Begin by assembling the inner shelves (B) and the inner posts (D). Line up the grain on the three shelves. Glue and dowel the same corner on all three shelves. Then glue the holes of one post and push the shelves snug (see figure 8). Add the other two posts in the same way. Clamp across the shelves as needed to keep the joints closed, but make sure that the weight of the clamps doesn't pull the structure out of square. Keep checking that the shelves and posts remain square as you go.

4. Place the base on some blocking so that clamps will fit under it. Glue and assemble the joints between the inner posts and the base, and between the inner posts and the top shelf. The grain of the top shelf should run in the same direction as that of the inner shelves. You must balance the position and pressure of the clamps you apply to keep the posts square to the base. Be patient, and beware of applying too much pressure.

5. Glue and dowel the outer posts in place by inserting their bottom ends first and then pushing them up to the top shelf. Clamp lightly and check the right angles at the base again. There! You're done! Move the plant stand by lifting the base, and give yourself a pat on the back—just not at the same time.

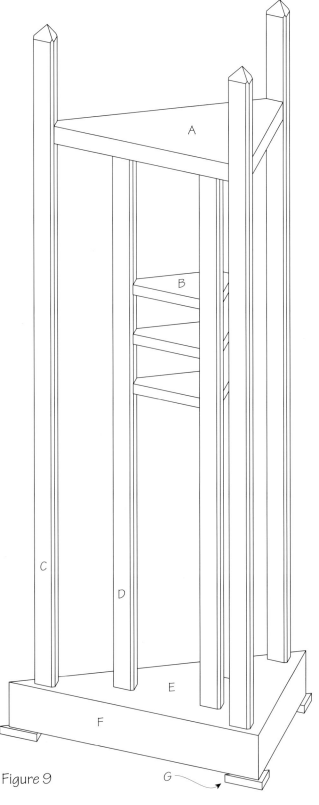

Figure 9

Bent Apron Table

DESIGNED BY RICHARD JUDD

This elegant table has a traditional feel with clean, contemporary lines. As you can see, Richard Judd combines a bubinga or cherry top with black lacquered legs and apron for strong contrast. You might substitute wenge for the base. Or try birdseye maple for the top with a cherry base, for an even more traditional look.

Materials

4/4 bubinga

12/4 poplar

3/8" lauan bending plywood

1/8" birch bending plywood

Supplies

Table top fasteners

3/4" MDF or particle board

Cutting List

CODE	DESCRIPTION	QTY	MATERIAL	DIMENSIONS
A	Top	1	bubinga	3/4" x 22" diameter
B	Inner apron	3	lauan bendply	3/8" x 3½" x 52"
C	Outer apron	1	birch bendply	1/8" x 3½" x 52"
D	Legs	4	poplar	2¾" x 2¾" x 25¼"
E	Tenons	8	poplar	3/8" x 2" x 2⅜"

MAKING THE TOP

1. Flatten and thickness enough material for the top (A). (See Flattening, Thicknessing, and Jointing on page 8 to review the process.) Arrange the boards and joint the adjacent edges. (Refer to Gluing Table Tops on page 10 for helpful tips.) Glue the edges and clamp up using double pipe clamps or alternating single clamps. Make sure the top is flat, and adjust the clamps if necessary.

2. When the glue has cured, scrape off any excess glue, and sand the faces flat. Working on the bottom side, draw a 22"-diameter circle. Cut to the line with the band saw. Remove the saw marks with a belt sander, working carefully to keep the edge square with the faces and to produce a true circle.

3. With a ball-bearing-guided 45° chamfer bit in the router, bevel the bottom edge to 1/4" from the top face.

4. Sand the top to 220 grit or finer. Keep the corners of the bevel sharp.

MAKING THE APRONS

1. To make the bending form for the aprons, cut five 18" squares from 3/4" MDF or particle board. Glue them together in a stack 3¾" high, using plenty of clamps. Draw a 17"-diameter circle on the stack, and band saw carefully to the line.

2. Cut the three inner aprons (B) from 3/8" lauan bending plywood, and cut two outer aprons (C) from 1/8" birch-faced bending plywood. The second outer apron is merely a clamping pad to protect the outer face of the apron.

3. If you have structural epoxy in your shop, use it for laminating the aprons. (See Structural Epoxy on page 19 for a short guide.) Otherwise, yellow woodworking glue will work as well, and these instructions assume its use. It's a good idea to make a notched glue spreader to speed the gluing process. Use a small piece of the 1/8" bendply, say 3" square, and band saw about 1/8" into one edge every 3/16" or so along the entire edge. Get out your band clamps, either one wide one or two or three 1" bands. Adjust them so that they form a circle at least 2" larger, all around, than the gluing form. Cut a 4"-wide strip of heavy plastic film the length of the aprons. Put a sheet of plastic film under the bending form. Make a stack in the following order: ⅛" bendply face up, plastic film, ⅛" bendply face down, three layers of ⅜" bendply.

4. Flip the first piece of bendply over next to the stack, and start spreading glue. You can spread it thinly on both faces, or more thickly on one face. Lauan bending plywood tends to absorb a lot of glue, so look for dry areas and give them more. Keep flipping a new layer onto the glued stack until the good face of the ⅛" bendply is up. Then flip the plastic and ⅛" clamping pad together on top of the stack. It is possible to wrestle the stack inside a band clamp and then slip it onto the bending form. You can also temporarily bar-clamp the middle of the stack to the side of the form while you string the webbing around the ends of the stack and pull everything together. However you do it, work quickly. Clamp the layers very tightly. Let the glue cure overnight if you can stand it.

5. Joint one edge of the apron until it is flat and the layers are even. If you can't do this on your particular jointer, clean up one edge with a sharp hand plane. Rip the apron to 3" wide on the table saw.

6. You will need to make a fixture to hold the apron while you cut its ends and joints. Glue up a stack of plywood 3" thick and 10" square. Cut two adjacent sides of the stack straight and square. Measure out from the corner of those two sides 9⅜" along both

sides. From those points square a line in and mark across it at 1". (See figure 1). Trace the outside of the apron to connect these two points. Band saw to the line, this time on the inside of the circle.

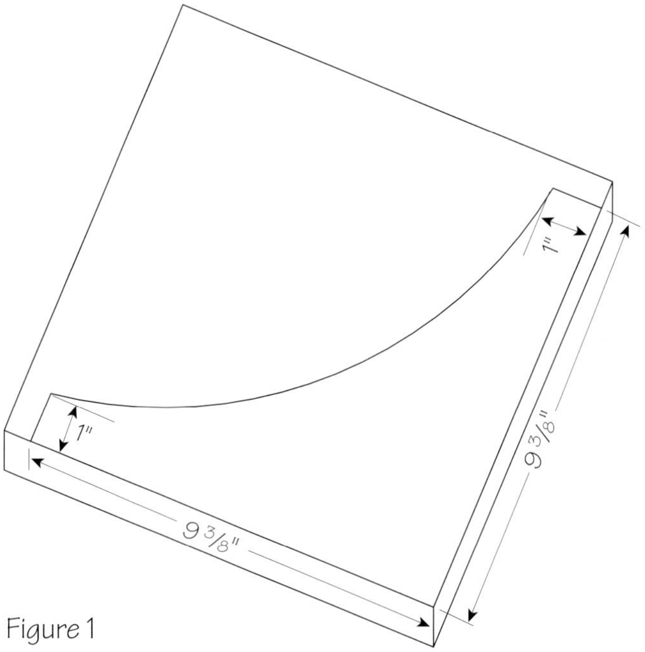

7. Measure around the outside of the apron to find the middle of its length. Cut it in half. Set the drop stop on your table saw to 9⅜" from the near side of the blade. (Refer to Drop Stops, Jigs, and Fixtures on page 12 for help.) Put the square corner of your plywood fixture against the drop stop, and cut off the extra length on that side. Turn the fixture, and trim the other arm. Hold a piece of apron against the fixture. Cut off one end of the apron to square it, then turn the apron, match its end to the top end of the fixture, and cut it to length. Be sure to support the large, cut-off end of the apron blank. Match the sawn end of that piece to the top end of the fixture as before, and cut the second apron piece to length. Repeat this process to produce two more aprons.

8. Use a biscuit jointer to cut two slots for table top fasteners near the top edge of each apron, centered about 2" from each end. Set the fence on the biscuit jointer to cut a slot slightly farther from the top edge of the apron than the inside height of the fastener. See photo 1.

MAKING THE LEGS

1. Rip the 1¾ stock for legs (D) into squares roughly 3" on a side. Flatten two adjacent faces, then thickness the squares to 2¾". Using a drop stop, cut the legs to length, 25¼".

Figure 1

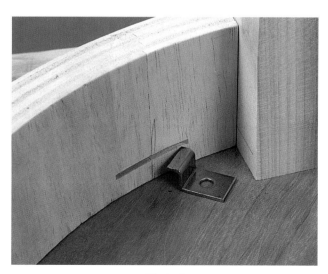

Photo 1

2. The outside face of each leg is straight, while the other three faces taper, as shown in figure 2. You could make jigs to taper the legs on the table saw (two jigs for the back and side tapers), but it is probably quicker to draw the tapers on the legs and band saw them. Draw the back taper on a side of each leg, from its top back corner to ¾" from the outside edge at the bottom. Band saw just outside the line, and clean the face with a pass over the jointer.

3. With the tapered back faces of the legs facing up, measure down 3¼" from their tops at each side. At the bottom end of each leg, mark 1" from each side. Connect the dots and band saw just outside the lines. Again, smooth the tapers on the jointer, but make sure that the tapers don't extend into the 3" joint area at the tops of the legs.

CUTTING THE JOINTS, ASSEMBLING, AND FINISHING

While these instructions follow Judd's practice of using loose tenons, you could join the aprons and legs with #20 biscuits. (See Biscuit Joinery on page 16 for an overview of the process.) The thickness of these aprons easily accommodates two biscuits per joint.

1. Cut ⅜" mortises, 2" wide and 1¼" deep, into the ends of the aprons. The mortises begin ⁷⁄₁₆" from the outside faces of the aprons. Use the plywood fixture to help hold the aprons during mortising.

2. Cut matching mortises in the legs, beginning ½" from the tops of the legs and ¹⁵⁄₁₆" from their outside faces, for a ½" offset between the outside faces of the legs and aprons.

3. Plane and rip a piece of poplar about 2' long for the tenons. Thickness plane the tenon stock to a sliding fit in the mortises. Round the corners to match the ends of the mortises, then cut the tenons to length.

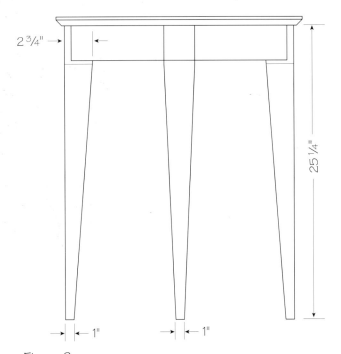

Figure 2

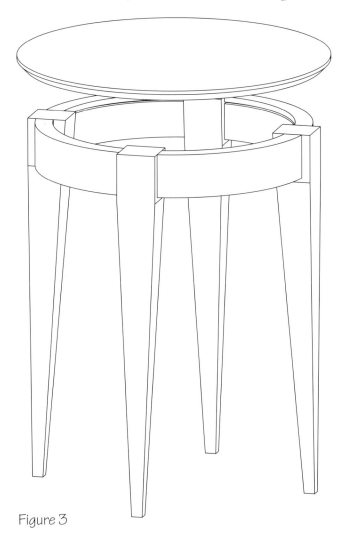

Figure 3

4. Assemble the legs, aprons, and tenons to make sure that the joints close well. If you need to make any adjustments, make sure you understand where the problem lies to avoid compounding the problem.

Photo 2

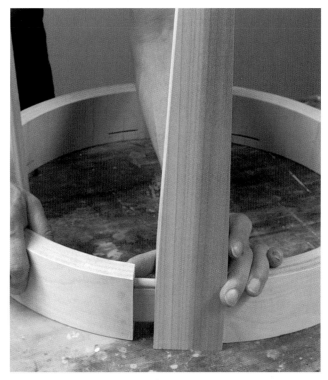

Photo 3

5. Sand the legs and aprons to 220 grit. Keep the joint areas of the legs flat. Ease all of the long-grain corners.

6. Reassemble the legs and aprons, with glue this time, and band-clamp everything snug. Make sure that the tops of the legs and aprons are flush.

7. Finish the legs and aprons with black lacquer, and the top with clear lacquer.

8. When the finish is perfect, lay the top on a padded surface, face down. Center the base on the top and drill pilot holes for the table top fastener screws. Drive those screws and you're done. Congratulations!

Photo 4

Macsai/Goren Dining Table

DESIGNED BY THOMAS STENDER

This table can seat 10 comfortably. Its lightweight appearance belies its Mission-style heritage. The wenge slats provide a sharp contrast with the cherry. You could use curly maple slats for a softer contrast. Be careful in changing its dimensions, because proportion is particularly important in this design.

Materials

4/4 cherry

3 x 3 cherry squares

6/4 wenge (or 4/4 wenge)

Supplies

#20 biscuits

#6 x 1" drywall screws

#10 x 4" drywall screws

3/16" washers

Cutting List

CODE	DESCRIPTION	QTY	MATERIAL	DIMENSIONS
A	Top	1	cherry	7/8" x 42" x 108"
B	Legs	4	cherry	2½" x 2½" x 28¼"
C	Long aprons	2	cherry	7/8" x 4" x 67"
D	Short aprons	2	cherry	7/8" x 4" x 25"
E	Stretchers	2	cherry	7/8" x 3" x 25"
F	Slats	24	wenge	3/8" x 1⅜" x 24¼"

MAKING THE TOP

1. Flatten, thickness, and joint 4/4 cherry for the top. (Refer to Flattening, Thicknessing, and Jointing on page 8 for tips on this process.) You will need to use extension rollers set to the heights of the infeed and outfeed tables to joint these planks. You want to achieve either dead straight or slightly concave edges with no humps. Press the jointed planks together, first by hand and then with clamps, to check for spaces in the joints. Normally, the toward-the-bark side of each plank will face down. (Review Gluing Table Tops on page 10 for more information.)

2. While the top is dry-clamped, measure its width in several places. Trim off excess material now, and straighten the outside edges of the top. You won't want to use anything but portable tools once it's glued together.

3. Make sure your working surface is flat. The tops of sawhorses, if you're using them, must lie in the same plane. Gather enough long clamps. Single pipe clamps, if you use them, must lie on alternate sides. Controlling planks of this length while you're gluing can be a struggle, so you may wish to use biscuits to help align the boards. Glue the joint edges and clamp up. Use a straightedge to make sure the top is flat. Adjust the clamps to correct any curves.

4. Draw pencil lines square across the ends, 108" apart, and trim the ends of the top carefully with a circular saw.

5. Sand all surfaces of the top to 220 grit or finer. You may as well begin applying a burnished oil finish (page 20) or another clear finish. You can finish the top completely while you work on the base.

MAKING THE BASE

1. Prepare the stock for the legs (B), and cut them to length using a drop stop (see Drop Stops, Jigs, and Fixtures on page 12).

2. Prepare the stock for the aprons (C and D) and the stretchers (E). Make these as thick as your material allows, then joint, rip, and cut them to length.

3. Mark the good side of each apron and stretcher. Use #20 biscuits to join the legs, aprons, and stretchers (see Biscuit Joinery on page 16 to review.) If your aprons and stretchers are ⅞" or thicker, use two biscuits in each joint, setting the jointer fence to ¼" and ⅝", working from the good side of the piece. Center the slots widthwise on each end of every apron and stretcher.

4. Mark the outsides of the legs, and determine their positions around the table. On both inside faces of each leg, draw a line 2" from the top end. On the inside face that joins a short apron (D), draw a line 5½" from the bottom of each leg (see figure 1). Those marks are the centerlines for cutting biscuit slots in the legs. Move the fence on the biscuit jointer ¼" farther from the blade for these leg slots. If you cut two slots in the apron ends, as described in step 3, set the fence at ½" and ⅞". Cut the slots on the inside faces of the legs, with the outside faces against the fence.

5. Mark the positions for the countersunk screw holes on

Figure 1

the bottom edges of the apron. On the long aprons (C), mark at 4" and 19" from each end and at the center (33½"). On the short aprons (D), mark at 3" from each end and at the center (12½"). Mount a ⁵⁄₆₄" bit in your drill press and set the depth stop to cut holes ending 3⅜" from the table. Bore those holes at every mark. Switch to a ⁵⁄₁₆" bit and extend the holes through the top edge of the aprons.

6. Mark the top edge of one short apron (D) for the slat dadoes. You need 12⅜" dadoes on 1¼" centers. Rather than work with a bunch of 16ths, mark the center of the length of the apron. Then measure from the center ⁷⁄₁₆" in one direction or the other, depending on the position of your table saw's miter gauge. Lay the apron, good face down, on the table saw, with its bottom edge against the miter gauge. The end toward the saw blade indicates the direction toward which you will measure and mark six slots. (Read on, Gentle Reader, for all will be made clear presently.) From the ⁷⁄₁₆" line, mark a ⅜" dado, then a ⅞" space, repeating until you have six dadoes marked. Your last mark should be 5⁷⁄₁₆" from the end of the apron (see figure 2).

7. With a ⅜" dado blade in the table saw set to cut ⅜" high, set the drop stop on the miter gauge (see page 12) to cut the slot nearest the middle of the apron. Measure with the apron itself: with its good face down, move the apron along the miter gauge until the first marked slot lines up perfectly with the width of the dado blade. Then move the drop stop to the end of the apron. Lay all the short aprons and stretchers (D and E) face down within reach of the table saw.

8. Cut the first slot in your marked short apron. Turn it end-for-end (good face still down), push it against the drop stop, and cut the second slot, which should be ⅞" away from the first and on the other side of the center mark. Cut two slots in the other short apron

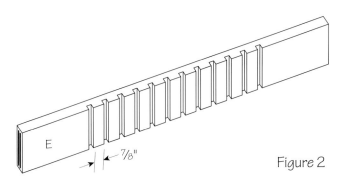

Figure 2

122

and in both stretchers. Now wasn't all that planning worthwhile? Only five more drop stop sets to go!

9. Using your marked short apron, set the drop stop to cut the next slot. Continue setting and cutting until you have 12 slots in each short apron and stretcher.

10. Clamp a fence ¾" from a ⁵⁄₆₄" bit in the drill press. Using a square, mark a line on the fence even with the center of the drill bit. With the slots facing up, drill two holes in the center of each slot through the short aprons and stretchers, each hole ¾" from an edge of the piece.

11. Mount a ⅜" countersink on the ⁵⁄₆₄" bit, turn the stretchers and short aprons over, and drill countersinks about ³⁄₁₆" deep, using the ⁵⁄₆₄" holes as guides.

12. While you're at the drill press, cut plugs from scrap cherry for all those countersinks. If you're never going to look critically at the insides of the short aprons, just make enough plugs for the stretchers. The four-pronged kind of plug cutter works best.

13. Sand the faces and edges of the long and short aprons and the stretchers to 220 grit. Sand the faces of the legs to 220, as well. You can finish these pieces now, but leave the area around the countersinks on the inside faces of the short aprons and the stretchers unfinished.

MAKING THE SLATS AND COMPLETING THE TABLE

1. Cut enough ⅘ wenge 25" long to make the 24 slats (F). You can figure ½" per slat, so you'll need at least 12" of width, measured in ½" increments. (If you must use ⅘ wenge, you will need to cut the slats in pairs from ripped 1⅜"-wide pieces.) Flatten, thickness to 1⅜", and joint the edges of the wenge.

2. Cut one end of each piece square. At that end of each piece, trace a ⅞"-radius quarter-circle on the edge, connecting the end and one face. Using the band saw, with the pieces on edge, saw close to this line to round the face into the bottom end of the slats. Use a low-angle block plane and sandpaper to smooth the curve. Sand the faces of the wenge pieces to 220.

3. Set the rip fence on the band saw ⁷⁄₁₆" from the near side of the teeth. Feeding slowly enough to keep the blade from wandering, rip one slat from each edge of each slat plank. Joint both edges and rip two

more slats. Keep jointing and ripping until you have at least 24 slats.

4. Thickness plane the slats until they are no looser than a squeaky fit in the slots. Then sand them to 220, wasting as little thickness as possible. Make sure that they all fit into the slots, then finish them completely. Yes, I do know that the top ends of the slats haven't been cut.

5. Have you rubbed and waxed all the parts of the table (except the inside faces of the short aprons and the stretchers? I won't write one more word until you're done. There. Begin the glory part by assembling the ends of the base. On a padded surface, lay out the parts in their relative positions: one short apron (D), one stretcher (E), and two legs (B). Glue the leg slots and push in biscuits. Glue the apron and stretcher slots and push everything together. The top edge of the apron should be flush with the tops of the legs, and the bottom edge of the stretcher should be 4" from the bottoms of the legs. Clamp in line with the apron and with the stretcher. Use a straightedge to check that the inside faces of the legs are parallel with each other. When the glue has dried, or right now if you have enough clamps, assemble the other end of the base.

6. If you don't have clamps 6' long, do you have clamps that you can gang together to span the length of the base? Devise a clamping strategy before you start gluing. And then get a helper. Glue the leg and long apron slots as before, insert biscuits, and pull the base together. When the clamps are in place, check for gaps, and check the diagonals to square the base.

7. Measure from the bottoms of the stretchers to the tops of the short aprons at all four end slots. The distance will be very close to 24¼". If you find a difference between the measurements, choose the smallest number and set the drop stop on your table saw miter gauge to that distance. Cut the top ends of all the slats (F).

8. Position a slat in a pair of slots so that the rounded edge is out and the rounded end is flush with the bottom of the stretcher. Hold it in place with a pair of spring clamps. Using a ³⁄₃₂ bit in your hand drill, bore a pilot hole, through a clearance hole in the stretcher, into the edge of the slat. Drive a #6 x 1" screw. Drill and drive a screw through the apron in the same way. Unclamp, then install screws in the remaining two holes for that slat. Repeat this procedure for all the slats.

9. Dip the rounded end of each plug in a puddle of glue and push it into a countersink, seating it with a tack hammer. When the glue has dried, carefully pare off the excess plug with a sharp chisel. Don't try to whack the whole thing off at once: if you guess wrong about the grain direction, you'll end up with a hole instead of a fill.

10. Sand the plugs to 220, then finish the inside faces of the short aprons and the stretchers.

11. You might want to attach the base to the table top in your dining room. If there's no carpet, put down some towels or other padding before you lay the top (A), good side down, on the floor. Are you sure that the bottom of the table top is facing up? Put the base assembly upside down on the top, centering it both ways. Push a ³⁄₁₆" washer into each hole in the aprons. Use a pencil or a long awl to mark the holes on the bottom of the top. Move the base diagonally until you can drill ⁵⁄₃₂" pilot holes ½" deep in the top. Drop one or two screws into the holes to make sure they weren't drilled too deep. Avoid marring the top as you put the base back in position. Drive the screws. Now all you have to do is find someone to help turn the table over. Oh! Get the vacuum and clean up that drilling dust. Good boy.

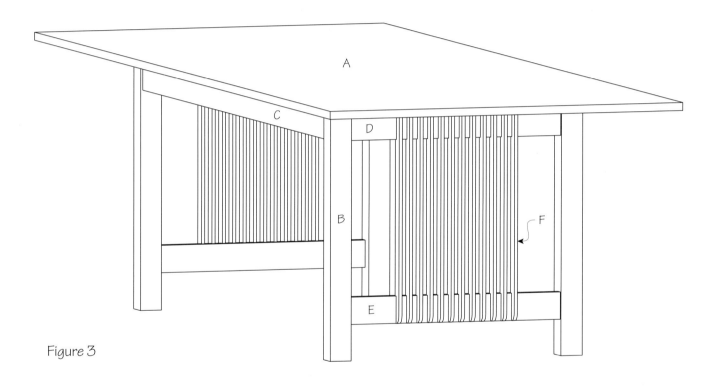

Figure 3

Acknowledgments

Although only one name appears on the front of this book, many people contributed to its successful completion. Their time and talent have made this book possible.

John Bickel, Richard Judd, Gary Peterson, Mark Taylor, and Ron Trumble generously made their designs available, patiently endured my requests for further information, provided slides and drawings, and answered my questions. I especially appreciate their contributions because I know how much such interruptions can detract from the joys of designing and making furniture.

Deborah Morgenthal guided my journey, pulled me through the rocky fords, and kept my wagon wheels aligned. She applied her editorial skills with gentleness, intelligence, and wit. I appreciate her example of clarity and calm good sense.

Kathy Holmes has created a design that allows the tables to shine. Her unflappable good will has been a comfort and an inspiration to me. She has listened patiently to my garbled ideas and read my mind. Most important, it must now be acknowledged that she did, in fact, have all the slides and only the slides she was supposed to have.

Evan Bracken tolerated, with good humor, my requests to consider ever one more possibility. He paid attention to the idiosycracies of each table, and strove to showcase them in his photographs. He even accepted with equanimity the extent of my photographic contribution, learned from King Lear: "More light!"

Leslie Bennis, of Asheville, NC, and Patti Quinn Hill and Thais Wiener, both of Weaverville, NC, graciously allowed us to use their lovely homes for photographic environments. I appreciate their patience as they watched us trample their rugs, rearrange their furniture, and endanger their decor. And I thank each of them for providing fine weather for photography.

Contributing Designers

From 1947 until 1979, **John Bickel** produced photographic illustrations for advertising. During those years, he also built his own home and a separate woodworking studio in Ossining, NY, and designed small sculptural objects, furniture, and some architectural work. He has been designing and making furniture full time since 1979.

Richard Judd received a degree in architecture from the University of Wisconsin, Milwaukee, in 1975. He has been a full-time furniture designer and maker since 1979. Judd uses an architect's eye to create elegant, contemporary furniture in his Paoli, WI, studio.

Gary Peterson was born in Pasadena, CA, a city rich in Arts and Crafts-style homes and furniture. In 1993, he brought his shop to Asheville, NC, where he has devoted his attention to adaptive development of this style. He employs basic hand-cut joinery, and usually uses traditional white oak in his designs.

Self-taught in woodworking and design, **Thomas Stender** has been making furniture since 1976. He fashions one-of-a-kind and limited edition pieces in a lyrical, wittily romantic style that has been called "Shaker on acid." His Ph.D. in English provides plenty of mind-fodder during long hours of sanding. Stender now designs furniture and household products for several manufacturers; edits, writes, and illustrates books about woodworking; and continues to make furniture in his Buffalo, NY, studio.

Mark Taylor started making furniture professionally in 1987 by reproducing traditional Shaker and Mission-style pieces. Lately, influenced by Josef Albers and Vassily Kandinsky, his work has evolved to incorporate more geometric elements while retaining the basic lines of the Shaker and Mission styles. He maintains a studio in Gallatin, TN.

While **Ron Trumble** was opening a woodworking studio in New Rochelle, NY, in 1979, he was also the understudy for a lead in the Broadway production of *Children of a Lesser God*. Now located in Berkeley, CA, Trumble is just as busy. He is a member of Nexus, a nine-member woodworking cooperative, as well as owner of his one-person company, Trumblewood. His current designs are influenced by the work of Frank Lloyd Wright and Charles Rennie Mackintosh.

Metric Conversion Table

Inches	Centimeters		Inches	Centimeters
⅛	3 mm		12	30
¼	6 mm		13	32.5
⅜	9 mm		14	35
1/2	1.3		15	37.5
⅝	1.6		16	40
¾	1.9		17	42.5
7/8	2.2		18	45
1	2.5		19	47.5
1¼	3.1		20	50
1½	3.8		21	52.5
1¾	4.4		22	55
2	5		23	57.5
2½	6.25		24	60
3	7.5		25	62.5
3½	8.8		26	65
4	10		27	67.5
4½	11.3		28	70
5	12.5		29	72.5
5½	13.8		30	75
6	15		31	77.5
7	17.5		32	80
8	20		33	82.5
9	22.5		34	85
10	25		35	87.5
11	27.5		36	90

Index